Cost-Effective
Recipes for 10 to 100

Cost-Effective Recipes

CAROLYN BREEDING, M.S., R.D.

EPI Corporation
Richmond, Kentucky

for 10 to 100

DONNA FOSTER, R.D.

Shriner's Hospital
Lexington, Kentucky

VNR *Van Nostrand Reinhold*
_____ *New York*

Copyright © 1989 by Carolyn Breeding and Donna Foster

Library of Congress Catalog Card Number 88-21109

ISBN 0-442-22119-3

Printed in the United States of America

Text design by Kathryn Parise

Van Nostrand Reinhold
115 Fifth Avenue
New York, New York 10003

Van Nostrand Reinhold (International) Limited
11 New Fetter Lane
London EC4P 4EE, England

Van Nostrand Reinhold
480 La Trobe Street
Melbourne, Victoria 3000, Australia

Macmillan of Canada
Division of Canada Publishing Corporation
164 Commander Boulevard
Agincourt, Ontario M1S 3C7, Canada

16   15   14   13   12   11   10   9   8   7   6   5   4   3   2   1

Library of Congress Cataloging in Publication Data
Breeding, Carolyn, 1949-
     Cost-effective recipes for 10 to 100 / Carolyn Breeding, Donna Foster.
          p.   cm.
          Includes index.
          ISBN 0-442-22119-3
          1. Quantity cookery.   2. Menus.   I. Foster, Donna, 1940-
II. Title.   III. Title: Cost effective recipes for ten to one hundred.
TX820.B68   1989
641.5'7—dc19   88-21109
                                                                         CIP

CONTENTS

PREFACE

Time—what a precious resource! We all have the same twenty-four hours, but where does it go? As dietary managers know, recipes should be adjusted for the exact amount needed to insure fewer leftovers and lower food cost. Accurate recipes are central to successful food production, yet who has the time to adjust each and every recipe when resident population fluctuates? Adjustment of recipes is both difficult and time-consuming, and many cooks will not follow a recipe that is not in the correct form at the time of preparation. In *10 to 100* we have done this for you. Each recipe is adjusted to ten levels of production and can be easily utilized in terms of a fluctuating census.

In addition, each recipe has an analysis of carbohydrate, protein, fat, and sodium content to help in planning therapeutic diets, and to assure the dietary manager that the needs of each resident are being met.

As dietitians for many years, we have had the opportunity to try many different recipes and recipe formats. We believe this collection represents the finest of those we have used and the most convenient format we have developed. These recipes have proven popular with young as well as old, in small acute-care hospitals and long-term care facilities, are easy to prepare, and are cost effective.

Providing quality foodservice in health care institutions has long been a challenge to health care professionals. Rising food costs, expensive but unskilled labor, and time shortages for managers often make planning and implementing menus a major undertaking. Much of the success of the menu depends on the recipes. Since many of those responsible for actual preparation of the food are unskilled, recipes must be simple and concise. In addition, it is helpful to have recipes that contain only standard ingredients which are ordinarily found in stock and with which the cook is familiar.

In addition, we have included two three-week menu cycles that incorporate many of the recipes featured here. Other sections provide helpful hints on menu development and marketing, food production, and cost control.

It is our hope that this book will be a working cookbook—not one that is thumbed through occasionally and left on the shelf. The "proof of the pudding is in the sauce," and we think you'll be very pleased with the results of using recipes and menus from *10 to 100*.

PART I *Providing Quality Foodservice to Health Care Institutions*

CHAPTER 1   *Menu Development*

*M*enu planning can be an enjoyable, creative experience if properly organized and executed. Successful menu cycles are well accepted by both residents and the dietary staff who prepare them. To develop such a cycle certain preliminary decisions must be made based on input from several sources before the actual writing begins.

Defining the Market

The first step in successful menu planning is defining the market to be served. Who will receive these meals? Realizing the importance of this basic question is the key to proper planning. Consider the following areas:

Regional Food Preferences. Regional food preferences refer to foods common to and popular within a certain geographical area. These are foods or food combinations around which many of your residents planned their own menus—foods they feel comfortable with and enjoy. It is important to determine what these foods are and make them a part of your new menu cycle. A questionnaire is a useful tool to determine these regional preferences and can be a great resource for the planning process. An example of such a form is shown (Fig. 1-1), or one could be developed based on information desired.

The questionnaire can be incorporated into an activity program in long-term care facilities or can be distributed from time to time on patient trays. When residents feel a part of the menu planning process, acceptance of the menu is likely to increase.

In the event residents are unable to provide information concerning food preferences and dislikes, information can be obtained from family members either during the admission process or soon after. Individual tastes should be considered to the extent possible and will go a long way in promoting the individual's satisfaction with the food service.

FIGURE. 1-1   Questionnaire

Please circle foods you prefer for breakfast.

1) Eggs
    scrambled
    fried
    poached
    benedict
    creamed
    omelet

2) Sausage

3) Bacon

4) Dry cereal

5) Cooked cereal

6) Toast

7) Biscuits

8) Pancakes

9) Waffles

10) Donuts or danish

11) Gravy

Do you prefer: Light lunch, heavy supper, heavy lunch, light supper?

Suggestions for the lunch menu:

Suggestions for the supper menu:

Preferred lunch time _____ Supper time _____

Suggestions for evening snacks:

One of the most difficult tasks in the menu planning process is to add variety while still maintaining traditional foods that are well accepted.

Regional Menu Patterns.   Do the residents prefer the heaviest meal at noon or in the evening? Are they used to a "full breakfast" at sunrise or a continental breakfast at 9:00 A.M.? Are special menus expected on Sundays? These are questions that must be answered and considered during the menu planning process.

Here again a questionnaire might provide insight. Also consider the following:

1. Do the residents retire early? If so, they may prefer a light evening meal.
2. Are the residents active well into the evening, perhaps receiving visitors or participating in an activity? If so, they may need the heavier meal at this time or perhaps a substantial snack at bedtime (HS).
3. Does lunch follow soon after breakfast (3½ to 4 hours)? If so, residents may not be hungry for a large lunch, and lighter fare may be the answer.

If regional menu patterns are not well understood, meals will not be accepted simply because residents may not be ready for them and feel "out of sync" with the meal schedule.

Mobility, Physical Status, and Age of the Residents.   Other factors in successful menu planning include the physical condition and age of the population to be served.

Very ill, skilled-care residents require different menu consideration than those who are ambulatory and active. Menus designed for children and young adults will be different from those planned for the elderly because eating habits have changed significantly over the last thirty years.

Once the physical status of the residents is determined, it is advisable to check the recommended daily allowances (RDA) for the specific age group with which you are dealing so that adequate calories and nutrients will be incorporated in the menus. This information will also be vital in planning portion sizes.

Another consideration is the number of therapeutic diets to be served. If a large number of the residents require therapeutic diets, the menu planner will want to plan simpler meals consisting of foods that can be easily adapted for a variety of diets. In this way, regular menus can be easily modified to meet each patient's needs without placing undue strain on the dietary department. This is especially important when staffing or equipment is limited.

Evaluating Resources

Once the market is determined, it is time to evaluate other areas that will also impact on the planning process. These include equipment, staffing, budget, and availability of commodity foods.

EQUIPMENT

A menu cycle can be beautifully planned to meet all the needs and expectations of the market and still fail if the menu planner does not consider available equipment resources.

When planning meals, care must be taken to utilize several pieces of equipment and to avoid overload of any one appliance. An example of this can be seen in the following menu:

Baked Pork Chops
Scalloped Potatoes
Buttered Peas
Cornbread
Whole Baked Apples

Four of the five items in this menu require oven space, and unless several ovens are available, they may be impossible to prepare simultaneously. It is important to be aware of equipment availability at all times during the planning process with the result that all equipment is utilized efficiently.

STAFFING

A similar consideration must be given to dietary staffing. First, evaluate the staffing pattern. If your staffing is heavier for the morning shift, plan the heavier meals during this shift and have a lighter evening meal when staffing is reduced. If staffing on both shifts is equal, the choice can be made according to resident preference.

If resident preference is contrary to your present staffing pattern, consider altering your pattern. Try not to get into the habit of doing things because "we've always done it that way." Be receptive to new procedures and ideas that may increase the effectiveness of the department.

Consider staffing when choosing specific menu items as well. If only one cook is scheduled for breakfast, preparing fried eggs for each resident may prove extremely difficult. This in turn may result in a poorly prepared meal or in the cook ignoring the menu altogether and preparing something simpler.

Meeting with the dietary staff prior to menu planning may make it possible to avoid past mistakes and may yield valuable information. The end result can be greater menu compliance and fewer substitutions.

Dietary staff members will also be able to point out items from the present cycle that are not well accepted or difficult to prepare, thus allowing the menu planner to avoid these items on the new cycle.

BUDGET

The budgetary goals of the administration must be your goals as well. It would be foolish to begin a menu cycle without consideration of these goals and a plan to stay within financial boundaries.

Know how much you have to spend. A daily log of food expenditures is an invaluable tool. Weekly totals allow the manager to see both what she has spent and to calculate how much is still available.

Before beginning a new menu, take time to review food invoices and note any items that have become too expensive. Since market prices for food can fluctuate from month to month, this must be an ongoing procedure. Regular price review with appropriate menu adjustment keeps menus cost effective.

The menu planner must also be knowledgeable about price per serving. This figure may be much higher than it appears for some items. Chicken is a good example. At $.80/lb chicken appears to be an inexpensive entrée, but what does it actually cost to serve a piece of chicken? If an average chicken weighs 2½ lbs, the cost of each chicken is $2.00. Each chicken serves four people for an average portion cost of $.50. Compare this to a portion cost of $.26 for five (3 oz) servings of ground beef at $1.30/lb. Cost per serving cannot always be based entirely on cost per pound. Some meats, like chicken, have a high percentage of waste. Learn to think in terms of yield.

By the same token, a serving of fruit for dessert may cost double that of a serving of cake with icing. If the fruit is not necessary to meet the recommended daily allowance on a given day, cake is more cost effective. Less expensive desserts can be used to balance out more expensive entrées for some menus and to add variety to menus.

Each of these factors will impact on the food cost and are an integral part of the menu planning process.

USE OF COMMODITY FOODS

If the facility is eligible for commodity foods, these should be planned into the menu to assure proper utilization and to avoid waste and spoilage. Research may be necessary to obtain suitable recipes for these items to increase acceptance by residents.

An example of a commodity food that requires planning for proper utilization is raisins. If raisins are in good supply, they can be incorporated into the menu in the following ways:

Added to oatmeal for breakfast
In cookies, pies, or fruit salad
In sauces such as raisin sauce for ham
In muffins or bread
As a bedtime snack

Proper planning assures that commodity foods are used and not just placed in the store room to gather dust, or worse yet, to spoil.

Other common commodity food items are nonfat dry milk, cheese, dried eggs, butter, and dehydrated, instant potato flakes. These items are all basic to most food services and can be very useful as well as cost effective.

The USDA provides detailed information on use and storage of many commodity foods. Become knowledgeable about the use of these items and teach cooks to use them properly for best results.

Selecting a Cycle

Menu cycles may be as short as one week or as long as eight. The typical menu cycle, however, is three or four weeks. Length of cycle is often a matter of precedent—what are the residents and staff used to, or what is the personal preference of the menu planner. Whichever length is chosen, remember that it is difficult not to repeat menus once the cycle exceeds four weeks. A shorter cycle may actually provide as much variety since repetition can be more easily avoided.

A menu cycle can also be selective or nonselective. The primary advantage of a *selective* cycle is that it allows choices by the resident and so may be better accepted than a nonselective menu. These menus can also be more expensive to serve and result in increased cost for both labor and food. The *selective* cycle requires careful planning on the part of the manager to avoid waste and may require more food preparation and holding equipment.

Nonselective menus are cost effective for both food and labor but offer no choices by the resident and so might be poorly accepted

unless carefully planned. Resident input in the menu planning process may offset this to some degree. For instance, consider leaving blank one meal on the cycle. Residents can plan the menu for that meal each time it comes up on the cycle.

Meeting the RDAs

Once the preliminary decisions have been made, it is time to review the basic nutritional requirements that must be met for all residents.

VITAMIN A

Foods high in Vitamin A include dark green or deep yellow vegetables or fruits. Four servings of these foods per week meet the requirement for this vitamin since it is fat soluble and can be stored in the liver. Examples of foods high in Vitamin A include broccoli, greens, carrots, apricots, or yams. Two ounces of liver once a week will also meet the requirement.

VITAMIN C

One source of Vitamin C per day is necessary to meet the needs of most individuals. The best sources are citrus fruits such as oranges or grapefruits, but several other foods are also high in this vitamin. Strawberries and cantaloupe are two examples.

OTHER FRUITS AND VEGETABLES

Menus should be planned to include four servings per day including the Vitamin C and A sources mentioned above. In this category we find foods such as potatoes, corn, peas, peaches, and apples.

MILK

Milk requirements vary with age. Four cups per day are required for children and two cups per day for adults. If a patient does not drink milk, it is difficult to meet the calcium requirement with other dairy sources. For example, to replace one cup of milk the resident would have to eat two cups of cottage cheese or 1¾ cups of ice cream. Requesting a calcium supplement may be more appropriate as well as more practical.

MEAT AND PROTEIN FOODS

Five ounces of edible protein must be provided each day. Examples of foods and portion sizes that provide one ounce of edible protein include:

> 2 T Peanut Butter
> 3 Sausage Links
> ¼ C Cottage Cheese
> 1 Egg
> ½ C Cooked Dried Beans or Peas
> 1 oz Processed Cheese
> 4 Strips of Bacon
> 1 oz Cooked Meat, such as beef or chicken

BREAD AND CEREALS

Four or more servings per day from this group satisfy the requirements. A broad choice of foods are available, for example:

> 1 Slice of Bread, or 1 Roll
> 2 Squares of Graham Cracker
> 1 oz Dry Cereal
> ½–¾ C Cooked Cereal
> ½ C Cooked Rice, Macaroni, or Noodles

FATS

Three or more teaspoons of fat should be provided each day. This is usually satisfied by offering margarine with each meal but could also be met by adding it to cooked foods such as cereal and vegetables. Emphasis should be placed on vegetable fats rather than on animal fats such as lard.

Institutional Menus and the Dietary Guidelines for Americans

The dietary guidelines issued by the Department of Health, Education, and Welfare advise Americans to do the following:

> 1. Eat a variety of foods.
> 2. Maintain ideal weight.
> 3. Avoid too much fat, saturated fat, and cholesterol.
> 4. Eat foods with adequate starch and fiber.
> 5. Avoid too much sugar.
> 6. Avoid too much sodium.
> 7. Drink alcohol in moderation, if at all.

What does this mean to those of us who plan menus? Experience has shown that a resident population responds best to foods that are familiar. Familiar foods may include some items high in fat, sugar, or sodium. The menu planner must use common sense in restricting these in the regular diet. What purpose has been served if a meal meets these guidelines yet is consumed by less than 50 percent of the residents?

Favorite recipes that are well received by the resident poulation should not be removed from the menu. Several actions can be taken, however, to modify excessive consumption of fat, sugar, or sodium in ways that will not interfere with acceptance.

1. Recipes can be modified by substituting healthier alternatives for some recipe ingredients. Examples of this include substituting reconstituted nonfat dry milk for whole milk in cooking; substituting vegetable oil for animal fat, and eliminating or reducing the amount of butter or margarine added to vegetables, etc. By using margarine instead of butter, cholesterol consumption can be greatly reduced. Solid fats like margarine can be replaced with polyunsaturated oil (such as corn oil) by reducing the amount called for by 25 percent. For example, ¾ cup corn oil would replace one cup of margarine.

2. Salt in cooking can be eliminated or reduced and use of herbs and spices encouraged. Substituting low sodium products, such as low sodium soup, in cooking will also lower total sodium consumption.

3. Sugar can be reduced by 25 percent without loss of quality in most recipes.

4. By substituting egg whites for half the eggs in a recipe, cholesterol can be reduced since all the cholesterol in an egg is in the yolk.

5. When planning a meal particularly high in fat or starch, round out with green vegetables or salads and plan fruit for dessert. Moderation is the key.

6. Consider resident teaching. Prepare informative displays, address the resident's council, organize taste panels to sample new, healthful menu items.

Change is often difficult to achieve, particularly among long-term care residents. It is the menu planners' responsibility to meet recommended daily allowances through foods that are well accepted and enjoyed by those who receive them.

A menu planning chart (Fig. 1-2) can be used to determine that all RDAs have been met for each day of the menu cycle.

Aesthetic Factors

When all is said and done, the simple truth of menu writing is that the meal must look good to be good. Residents must be persuaded to try new menus, and it is here that aesthetic factors become important.

COLOR

Many different aspects of the appearance of the meal combine to make it look good or bad. First, contrast in color is necessary to prevent the meal from looking too bland. One food may determine the success or failure of the look. For example, consider the following menu:

Roast Pork with Gravy
Cornbread Dressing
Cabbage

This meal, although tasty, is colorless and bland. Cabbage is a poor choice for the vegetable because it provides no contrast in color. Peas would be a better alternative, particularly frozen peas that have been carefully prepared to preserve color and texture. With this menu change, the whole appearance of the meal is altered.

In some instances, when the menu writer is trying to plan for traditional combinations of food, this is a difficult rule to follow. A boiled dinner of corned beef, cabbage, and potatoes is traditional but colorless. In this situation a garnish may solve the problem of providing a contrast in color while preserving the traditional food combination. Two spiced apple rings or a sprig of fresh parsley would add color to the plate. A wide variety of garnishes is not necessary. A few, carefully selected items will compliment many meals. Examples of versatile garnishes include parsley, tomato slices or wedges, lemon, spiced apple rings, and leaf lettuce. Using a limited number reduces both storage problems and waste.

FIGURE 1-2   Menu Planning Chart

	No. Sources Vit. A	No. Sources Vit. C	No. Other Vegs/Frts	No. Serving Milk	Oz. Meat/Protein	No. Bread/Cereal	Fats
Day 1							
2							
3							
4							
5							
6							
7							
Total For Week I							
8							
9							
10							
11							
12							
13							
14							
Total For Week II							
15							
16							
17							
18							
19							
20							
21							
Total For Week III							

CONSISTENCY AND TEXTURE

Consistency and texture must also be considered. If cream of potato soup is served as an entrée, applesauce and ice cream would be poor accompaniments. All are of a similar consistency and texture and the menu lacks eye appeal and interest. Changes in the fruit and dessert are necessary to provide variety in consistency and texture. A revised menu might be:

> Cream of Potato Soup
> Tomatoes Vinaigrette on Leaf Lettuce
> Chocolate Brownie with Icing

The varying textures and consistencies add the variety needed.

SHAPE

Variety in the shape of the foods on the plate is also necessary to maximize eye appeal. Consider this menu:

> Fried Chicken Planks
> French-Style Green Beans
> Julienne Beets in Orange Sauce

All the foods are cut into strips, resulting in a less than pleasing combination. All that is needed are a few changes in the shape of the foods to make the menu acceptable:

> Fried Chicken
> French Style Green Beans
> Sliced Beets in Orange Sauce

TASTE

Certain flavor combinations compliment one another and have become traditional in menu writing—corned beef and cabbage, sausage and fried apples, hot dogs and baked beans are a few examples. When these foods are served together, each enhances the flavor of the other.

It is important to be aware of and to utilize these special combinations when planning a menu cycle. Each area of the country has certain flavor combinations that are unique to the area.

It is also important to consider what combinations of foods do not work. Avoid using too many foods of similar taste in the same menu. Balance out strong-flavored foods with bland foods. Use rich foods sparingly in combination with lighter, fresh-tasting foods.

Make your staff aware of the importance of aesthetic factors of food. Here are several suggestions for increasing staff involvement in this area:

1. Encourage the cook and dietary staff to taste food during preparation and make suggestions.
2. Develop a quality assurance program that has dietary staff members rating meals at periodic intervals.
3. Plan an inservice on aesthetic factors using examples from food magazines—"A picture is worth a thousand words!"

Additions to the Menu

A wise menu planner leaves nothing to chance. Good menus are complete and include all foods to be prepared by the department on any given day. This includes garnishes and nourishments.

GARNISHES

Garnishes should be carefully planned to assure that they are both appropriate and cost effective. Including them on the menu will accomplish the following:

1. Assure that the garnish compliments the meal. You might be surprised to find the cook may not choose appropriate garnishes when these are not specified.
2. Make ordering easier since it is clear what garnishes are needed for each meal.
3. Make certain that garnishes will actually be used since they are written as part of the menu.

NOURISHMENTS

Nourishments can be a tremendous drain on dietary finances if not carefully planned. Planning them into the menu is necessary to assure that the needs of the resident are being met in an appropriate manner. It assures that the nourishments will be ordered in a timely manner and be available when needed. It also enables the menu planner to avoid repetition in this area.

Before planning nourishments, take time to consider what the per serving cost will be. Remember that they must fit into the total budget for the day. It is also important to maintain good communication lines to determine if snacks are being accepted and to observe if they are being distributed appropriately.

Marketing the Menu

Once the menu cycle has been completed, reviewed with the staff, and recipes provided for new foods, there is a final step—marketing.

Marketing consists of "selling" the menu to the residents and the staff who will serve it. One important tool for this is the menu board. Consider the following menus:

Menu 1	Menu 2
Chicken Livers	Fried Chicken Livers
Mashed Potatoes	Whipped Potatoes with Cream Gravy
Peas	Buttered Peas
Biscuit	Homemade Biscuit
Cake	Chocolate Cake with Icing

Which meal sounds better? Which sounds more carefully prepared? Be aware of the impact the menu board can have and use it to your advantage. Menu boards are read by many people each day. Make sure that the spelling is correct and that the board is always up-to-date.

In long-term care facilities or similar situations where nursing departments may serve the meals, take time to discuss with those responsible for the service how the meals should be served. It is important that the server have a positive attitude and that comments about the meal that have a negative connotation are avoided.

In cases where the resident is fed or when the diet has been altered by consistency, the simple procedure of telling the resident what he is receiving may be beneficial. Staff enthusiasm can work miracles. Inservice the staff on correct feeding techniques and include this step as an important part of the feeding process. These techniques may also be worked into the orientation process for new employees.

CHAPTER 2 *Controlling Food Cost*

*C*ontrolling food cost is an increasing concern for today's foodservice manager. This concern is further complicated by the role of the dietary department in the care of the resident who requires a therapeutic diet and in attracting private paying residents to the competitive long-term care market. Dietary has become "big business." The era of the home-style kitchen is past, and the dietary department has become a significant cost cutter as well as a marketing tool.

Control of food cost has many different aspects but can basically be divided into five broad areas—purchasing, receiving, record keeping, production, and inventory control.

Purchasing

Purchasing is a very important aspect of the foodservice manager's job and carries the responsibility of placing the welfare of the department above personal preferences or friendships. The manager must constantly reevaluate decisions to assure that they remain appropriate in an ever-changing market.

To begin, vendors must be chosen. Pricing is not the only consideration in this decision. Purchasing is a complicated process that must be carefully planned.

PRIMARY VERSUS MULTIPLE VENDORS

Purchasing can be done with a primary vendor or from multiple suppliers. Arguments can be made for either procedure.

A primary vendor is one who meets almost all the needs of the food service. The foodservice manager buys as much as possible (usually about 80 percent of purchases) from a single supplier, thereby maximizing volume and lowering prices. This may be especially helpful for small facilities.

Use of a primary vendor reduces the amount of time spent in ordering and receiving since purchases are with a single company. A primary vendor may also be more willing to work with the manager on obtaining new products or carrying a specific product line since the food company is assured of the account. Primary vendors may also offer special services such as menu analysis or costing at a nominal charge.

Using several vendors allows the manager to take advantage of competition between food companies to obtain lower pricing. Deliveries may be spaced at more convenient intervals. Continual price comparisons may also prevent price "creeping."

Another possible option in purchasing is to join or form a group-purchasing organization. Being part of a group whose total purchasing power is greater than that of each of the members results in more purchasing clout and lower pricing.

On the other hand, each member of the group may sacrifice the right to make individual decisions pertaining to selection of vendors or other related factors. Group purchasing has become popular in recent years and is available in many areas. To locate a purchasing group, try contacting the state organization for your particular field, such as the association of Health Care Facilities for long-term care units or the Hospital Association for acute-care facilities in your area. Dietitians may also obtain leads by contacting the state consultants organization.

OBTAINING THE BEST PRICING

Once the manager has decided whether to use one vendor or several, care must be taken to obtain the best possible pricing.

Bids

Bids are the best way to obtain formal price quotes of food and supplies. Use of this procedure assures the manager that vendors are quoting items of equal quality. Be aware that some vendors lower prices to gain an account. Once the account is established, prices slowly climb. Reviewing prices monthly will make this trend obvious. Be suspicious of vendors who offer prices considerably below those of competitors. Pricing may be best controlled by receiving price bids for specified periods of time such as one month or one year. This reduces the amount of time spent comparing prices between vendors. Bid prices are always confidential, and one vendor's price should never be revealed to another. Few prices are guaranteed for as long as a year, although it might be possible to obtain such an agreement on items such as bread, milk, or chemical supplies.

Payment Terms

It is always good to discuss how the company will bill and at what intervals. Some vendors expect payment within thirty days but may offer a discount to customers who pay earlier.

Payment terms may be a bargaining tool if the cash flow of the purchaser allows payment within seven days. Early payment is very attractive to some vendors and may qualify the buyer for lower pricing than usual. If this is an option for your facility, discuss the possibility with the potential food vendors when taking bids. Some food companies will also offer price breaks based on volume. For example, for each $1,000 of food or supplies purchased, the vendor may offer an additional price break such as 1 to 2 percent.

When bargaining for the best prices, consider all options!

ADDITIONAL CONSIDERATIONS IN CHOOSING A VENDOR

A review of the company's product list will allow the manager to decide whether the vendor carries the range of products needed. This is especially important when choosing a primary vendor because the manager may not be able to fall back on another vendor.

The quality of a company's products is best determined by a can cutting, comparing one company's products with those of competitors. Some food companies may offer to perform this service at their own warehouse or would at least donate samples of their products for testing. Can cuttings allow the manager to compare products from competing vendors firsthand.

DELIVERY SCHEDULE

The delivery schedule must be discussed to determine whether the company can provide the number of deliveries the facility needs at a time convenient to the facility and within a time frame that promotes neither overstocking or understocking.

Delivery scheduling can also be a bargaining point. By reducing the number of deliveries to the minimum, the vendor may be able to reduce the cost, and in return reduce pricing for the purchaser.

PURCHASING TECHNIQUES

Once a vendor has been chosen, the manager must establish good purchasing techniques.

1. Limit the personnel who purchase to the manager and her assistant. Make sure anyone assuming the responsibility even temporarily is trained not to deviate from established procedures.
2. Use a purchase order form to record orders. This can also be used to check incoming orders and to assure that the order received matches the order placed.
3. Always use specific item numbers for items to be purchased or specify quality desired. Do not allow the sales representative to choose for you. Be specific!
4. Do not become personally involved with sales representatives. Friendship with these individuals tends to carry an obligation to buy "at least something." The

buyer must be objective at all times about what is best for the company.

5. Consider placing orders by phone. This may be another bargaining point since it makes a salesman unnecessary, thereby reducing vendor cost. It also reduces the amount of time necessary to place orders and eliminates "visiting" with the sales representative.

Receiving

Once the order has been properly placed it must be properly received. There is much more to receiving than signing the invoice or putting the stock away. Lack of control in this area can cost major dollars. Consider this example:

A foodservice manager orders a 20-lb beef roast at $2.40 per lb for a total cost of $48. When the order is delivered the cook is busy, fails to check the order properly, and does not notice that the beef roast is not on the truck. The invoice is signed and the facility is charged $48 for the roast it did not receive. When roast comes up on the menu, the manager does not have one on hand and has to order another at an additional cost of $48. Failure to check the order properly has cost the facility $96.

When an order arrives, the manager or assistant should check the incoming stock against the purchase order form. These should match exactly. Do not allow the vendor to substitute for items not in stock unless the terms of the exchange have been agreed upon beforehand. Here are some terms of right to exchange:

1. The vendor will only substitute an item of equal or higher quality at the same price as the item being replaced.
2. The vendor will call the manager prior to delivery for notification of a shortage and to get authorization for a substitute.

3. The manager has the right to refuse any substitution and subtract the charge from the invoice.

On delivery of meats and produce sold by weight, products should be weighed to verify correct quantities. There are scales available for this that cost less than $100 and may quickly pay for themselves.

Do not sign the invoice unless the order is correct or corrections have been made in writing. Once signed the invoice is proof that the purchaser has accepted the order, and the vendor has no further obligation to credit items shorted, etc. if not noted. At some point soon after delivery, before turning invoices in for payment, the manager should check all prices against prices quoted at the time of purchase. Notes should be made of any errors or credits due and the vendor contacted. Procedure for credits should be established in advance.

STORAGE

Prompt storage of stock is important to assure safety and quality of the food supply. When stock is put away, the new stock should be placed behind the existing stock so the oldest is used first. Some companies find it helpful to price each item at this time for ease in inventory later.

The stock room should be organized for easy utilization. Similar items should be stored together, and shelves should be labeled if possible. Storing heavy items on lower shelves is an important safety consideration. Frequently used items placed near the entrance provide faster, easier access. A well-organized stockroom makes ordering and inventory faster and more accurate.

Record Keeping

One of the most crucial rules of cost control is "know how much you have to spend." In order to do so, and to avoid overspending, good records are a must. There are many significant figures relating to food cost, and each require different information and different methods of calculation.

MONTHLY FOOD EXPENDITURES

Many managers find it helpful to maintain a daily log of all food expenditures (Table 2-1). At the beginning of the month the amount budgeted for the month is logged. Delivery date, vendor, invoice number, and amount of each food invoice are recorded for invoices received each day. The amount of each invoice can then be subtracted from the previous total. The total of this calculation is the amount remaining for the month.

It should be noted that this type of a record does not differentiate food and supply purchases. If necessary these can be easily kept separate by requesting separate invoices for nonfood items. Some companies take this a step further by having the vendor separate invoices for paper items, dishwashing and cleaning supplies, and other supplies such as dishes and silverware. Decisions concerning this type of breakdown can be made based on individual company policy. Some companies do not require such detailed records from the dietary department. A wise manager however, knows how her budget dollars are spent and in what area.

Calculating Food Cost

Food cost cannot be adequately controlled if it is not monitored and feedback given to appropriate personnel. One of the simplest methods for calculating monthly food cost is shown in Figure 2-1. To utilize this form, it is necessary to take inventory of all food supplies at the beginning of the first month. Do not count paper or chemical supplies.

TABLE 2-1   Daily Log of Food Expenditures (beginning balance $6,500)

Date	Vendor	Invoice #	Amount	Total
2/4 $6,061.05	XYZ	42728	$438.95	
2/5 $6,045.69	Bread company	246	$ 15.36	
2/5 $5,919.35	Milk company	1776	$126.34	

FIGURE 2-1   Monthly Report of the Food Service

	(month or period)	year
Beginning inventory value		$_____
Cost of foods received during the month (purchased and donated)		_____
Value of food available during the month (A plus B equals C)		_____
Closing inventory value (Inventory value at the end of month)		_____
Cost of food used during the month (C minus D equals E)		_____
Total meals served during the month (Employees and residents)		_____
Average meal cost (Divide E by F to get G)		_____
Average per person per day food cost (Multiply G by 3)		$_____

This figure will be the "beginning inventory value." On the last day of the month, or as close to this date as possible, the inventory is taken again. This is the "closing inventory value."

"Cost of foods received" is the total amount spent on food from the first day of the month through the last.

After the first month, it is only necessary to inventory at the end of the month since the beginning inventory value for the second month will be the same as the closing inventory value of the preceding month.

To utilize this form it is necessary to keep an accurate meal census to record both patient and staff meals for the month. Such a record takes only a few minutes a day and is essential in calculation of food cost. This same form can also be utilized to calculate per person per day cost of all nonfood items.

FOOD COST BREAKDOWN

Food expenditures fall into several major categories—meats, vegetables, bread, milk, etc. In working with food cost figures it is often helpful—and enlightening—to know how food expenditures are divided. By dividing food expenditures into categories, the manager can see what percentage of the food dollar is spent in each area. This is useful in several ways.

First, by determining what percentage is spent on meats, milk products, etc., the manager can compare cost with standards in that particular area—hospital, nursing home, etc.

Another possible use is identifying problem areas. For example, if meat expenditures usually average 30 percent of the total food dollar, a manager would have cause for concern if this area jumped to 40 percent.

It is often difficult to pinpoint and explain sudden fluctuations in food cost. A food cost breakdown sheet makes this task easier. Figure 2-2 is an example of such a sheet, or one can be designed to fill your particular needs.

An accurate cost report should include all costs incurred in a given month. It never works to "hold over" invoices to the following month.

When keeping a monthly expenditure record always remember that a portion of the purchases for each month remains in inventory.

Using monthly expenditure records without considering the amount left in inventory gives a false picture of the food cost.

PER PATIENT DAY COST

Many managers prefer to consider per patient day cost. This can be calculated by using the form given in the section "calculating monthly food cost." This form also yields the cost per meal. A similar record can be kept for nonfood expenditures.

PRODUCTION TECHNIQUES

Food production begins with the menu itself. A good menu will tell the cook what to prepare, appropriate substitutions for therapeutic diets, and what portion size will be required for each item. It may also give recipe numbers and contain production information such as instructions for thawing items for the next day's meal.

Controlling Cost with Menus

The menus should be specific about what is to be cooked for each diet. This prevents individual interpretation which is sometimes costly and inaccurate. Portion sizes for each menu item should be stated in terms which correspond with the serving utensil to be used. For example

1 egg—#16 dipper
Vegetable—#8 dipper (or 4 oz spoodle)
Cooked cereal—6 oz ladle

The serving size for meats should be listed in ounces. In cases where meats must be sliced, a commercial meat slicer should always be used. Before the entire piece of meat is sliced, several representative

FIGURE 2-2   Dietary Food Cost Breakdown

Month of _____   Total for Month _____
Facility   _____

Date	Meat	Milk	Ice Cream	Eggs	Frozen Food	Produce	Bread	Canned Veg	Canned Fruit	Misc.
Totals										
%										

slices should be taken, weighed, and the slicer adjusted to the correct thickness for the portion size desired. For instance, if a four ounce serving of ham is specified there are three alternatives for slicing: one 4 oz slice, two 2 oz slices, or four 1 oz slices. In general, several thinner slices are more attractive and easier to chew (if this is a consideration). Several slices allow better plate coverage.

Other Portioning Tools

Scoops or Dippers. The number on each scoop refers to the number of scoopfuls necessary to make one quart. Remember that this is a level measurement. Sloppy use of scoops can cost money. Scoops are versatile due to the wide range of sizes available and ease of use. Holes drilled in the scoop bowl allow vegetables to drain. In addition to vegetables, these utensils are excellent for portioning cookies, meatballs, pudding, and some salads.

Spoodles. Spoodles are a cross between the traditional scoop and a ladle. They are generally sized according to ounce capacity and come both solid and perforated. The long handle prevents the utensil from slipping into the food.

Ladles. Ladles are sized according to ounce capacity and are excellent for soups, stews, or gravy.

Individual salad molds and custard cups allow exact portioning while providing an attractive shape and appearance.

Muffin tins are useful for cupcakes, rolls, and muffins.

Pie markers and cake markers make it possible to cut exact portions for these items.

The importance of standardized portions cannot be overemphasized. In addition to contributing to cost control, they are key factors in customer satisfaction with serving sizes, assure the manager that recipe yield will be reliable, and that each customer or resident will receive the amount of food he needs as part of his recommended daily allowances.

Production

Production sheets allow the manager to give written, specific instructions to each cook. There are many kinds in use and an example of one is Figure 2-3. Basically, production sheets give the cook instructions on topics such as what food to prepare, how long it should be cooked, how much of each food to prepare, and what should be done for the next day. This sheet is especially useful in controlling factors such as the number of cans of a vegetable to be opened or how many meat patties to prepare. If special diets are served, the sheet is particularly important because many cooks will not take time to count the number of servings necessary for low sodium diets, diabetic diets, etc. Knowing the exact number of each diet to be served is crucial to cost control. Production sheets are also effective in reducing leftovers and waste.

Standardized Recipes

Standardized recipes are essential in a well-run food service. In addition to insuring quality control, they also contribute to cost containment. Using standardized recipes, a manager knows exactly what to order for each recipe. The cook has specific instructions for each item on the menu and can prepare foods with which she may not be familiar and still obtain a quality product. This becomes especially important when training a new cook who is not familiar with the menu. With standardized recipes the quality of the food will be the same no matter who is cooking and leftovers will be minimized.

Any recipe can be standardized. If a particularly talented cook insists she has a better recipe than the one being used, ask her to bring it in. Test the recipe the next time it comes up on the menu and, if it is better, standardize it! Some of the best recipes are obtained in this way.

Standardizing a recipe is easy. Begin by preparing the recipe carefully, writing down any changes from the original ingredients or any change made in preparation technique. Try the recipe several

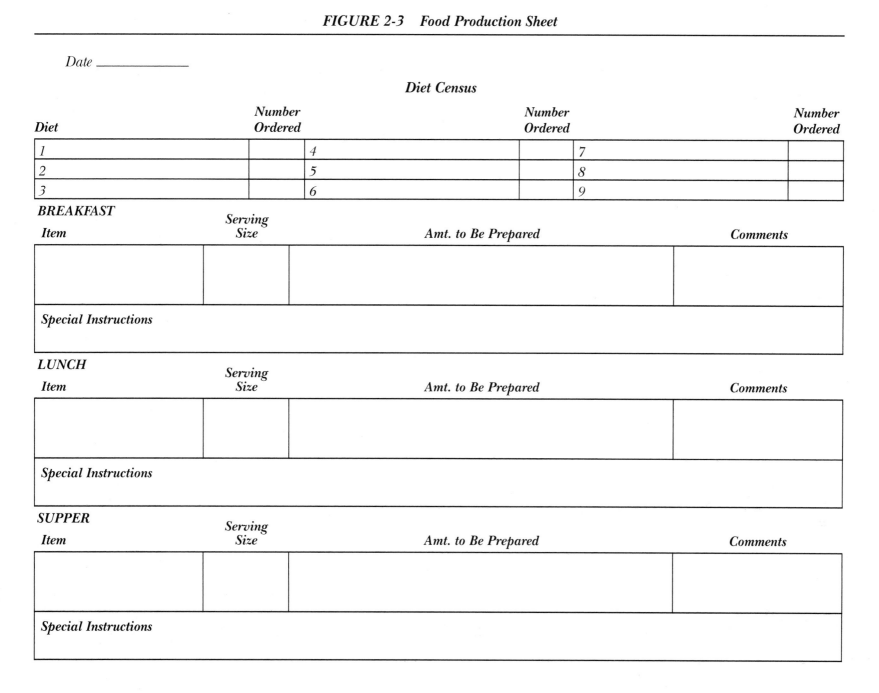

FIGURE 2-3 Food Production Sheet

Date _____

Diet Census

Diet	Number Ordered		Number Ordered		Number Ordered
1		4		7	
2		5		8	
3		6		9	

BREAKFAST

Item	Serving Size	Amt. to Be Prepared	Comments

Special Instructions

LUNCH

Item	Serving Size	Amt. to Be Prepared	Comments

Special Instructions

SUPPER

Item	Serving Size	Amt. to Be Prepared	Comments

Special Instructions

times, making any further adjustments necessary until the product obtained is satisfactory. Once this stage is attained, type or rewrite the recipe on the appropriate form, and place it in the working file. Each cook will use this recipe to prepare the item and it should yield a quality product each time.

Standardized recipes are most effective in cost control when adjusted to the exact amount needed. Many cooks have difficulty with this process, and it is often neglected since few recipes come adjusted to the correct amount. Another factor to be considered is the changing census in many long-term or acute-care facilities. The census today may be quite different from the census three weeks later when the cycle begins again, necessitating different amounts to be prepared. In *Cost Effective Recipes for 10 to 100,* this problem has been eliminated since the adjustment has already been done for a wide range of servings.

Supplements and Snacks

As mentioned previously, supplements and snacks can soon get out of hand. Supervision and control are key concepts in providing adequate between-meal nourishment without overly stressing the food budget.

Between-meal snacks should be planned on the menus and distribution of these snacks should be monitored and evaluated periodically. Standardized recipes should be used. In some states, regulations for long-term care require three snacks per day but in most situations, a bedtime snack is the only one routinely provided. This snack is especially important for insulin-dependent diabetics.

When providing three snacks per day, the morning and afternoon snacks are typically light and are usually fluids such as juice to prevent interference with meal consumption. Bedtime snacks tend to be more substantial and should contain a source of protein such as milk or cheese.

Whatever the situation, it is imperative that the manager monitor the program to see that, 1) the amount of snacks going out is adequate but not excessive. (It is not unusual to find any extra snacks going to

the staff); and 2) the time snacks are offered is appropriate. If the residents are already in bed and asleep, a bedtime snack is of no benefit. On the other hand, if passed too early, they will not be well accepted because the residents may not be hungry.

Supplement programs are often developed to add additional calories and nutrients to the diet of patients who are below ideal body weight or malnourished. As such, they are an important part of the resident's nutritional care.

While many facilities rely on commercially prepared supplements, these can prove very expensive and are often poorly taken. Home-made supplements can be very cost effective and much tastier than their commercial counterparts.

To use homemade supplements effectively, follow these guidelines:

1. Have the physician's approval if the supplement is replacing a commercial product.
2. Always use recipes.
3. Know what the product contains (nutritional analysis).
4. Prepare the product for immediate distribution to assure the best quality and the safest product.
5. Monitor the success of the program periodically to assess weight gain and individual tolerance and acceptance. Remove residents from the program when they have reached their weight range goal.
6. As with between-meal snacks, monitor distribution times and procedures.

The section on supplements in Chapter 8 contains recipes that are useful in providing additional calories and protein to residents who require extra nutritional support.

Inventory Control

A typical inventory may be worth several thousand dollars or more, depending on the size of the institution. The dietary manager is responsible for controlling what goes into inventory as well as what comes out.

A rule of thumb concerning inventory level is one half of food purchases for the month. Therefore, if a manager spends approximately $6,000 a month on food, the inventory should run about $3,000. This figure may increase in a month that has as additional delivery based on the length of the month and the day of delivery. If, for example, the institution receives a major food order every Tuesday, there will be several months with five Tuesdays rather than four. This additional expenditure should not increase food cost for the month because it is primarily held in inventory rather than actually used.

It is an accepted fact that the stock room should be kept locked and access to the area limited to prevent pilfering. This applies to inventory kept in freezers and cold storage as well.

CHAPTER 3   *Successful Recipe Production*

*I*t has been said that anyone who can read can cook. For this to be true, it is necessary for the cook to be able to read the recipe and to understand what it says. To do so, she must have knowledge of certain terms and procedures.

Using a Recipe for the First Time

When introducing a new recipe, always review it with those responsible for the preparation. Make sure all necessary ingredients are on hand and that the cook is familiar with cooking terms used in the recipe. This is a simple procedure, but necessary since many cooks will not indicate a lack of knowledge in this area for fear of seeming inadequate. Encourage each cook to try new recipes as an opportunity to learn new skills and techniques. The attitude of the manager can have a profound effect on development of this attitude in her employees.

Once the recipe has been reviewed, try to be on hand to taste and assess the completed product. Be honest in your evaluation and discuss any areas in need of improvement. Using this procedure, a recipe is not doomed for failure simply because of one bad episode.

Common Cooking Terms

A good inservice on common cooking terms will assist the dietary staff in interpreting recipes correctly. Some of the most frequently used terms are defined here for this use. Never assume that the staff is knowledgeable in this area simply because they have "cooked in dietary for years."

Baste	To moisten foods during cooking with pan drippings or with a special sauce to add flavor and prevent drying.
Beat	To make a mixture smooth by adding air with a brisk whipping or stirring motion using a spoon or electric mixer.
Boil	To cook in liquid to 212 degrees F when bubbles rise to the surface and break.
Braise	To cook slowly in a small amount of liquid in a tightly covered container—either on top of the stove or in the oven.
Chop	To cut into pieces about the size of a pea. May use a knife, blender, or food processor.
Coat	To evenly cover food with crumbs, flour, or batter.
Cool	To remove from the heat and let stand at room temperature. If the recipe states "cook quickly" the food should be placed in the refrigerator or walk-in cooler.
Cream	To beat with a spoon or electric mixer until soft and smooth. When creaming shortening and sugar, beat until light and fluffy.
Cube	To cut into square-shaped pieces of at least ½ inch.
Dice	To cut into small cubes of uniform size between ⅛ inch and ¼ inch.
Dot	To place small bits of food over another food such as dotting with butter before baking.

Fold	To add ingredients gently to a mixture using a spatula, cut through the mixture, cut across the bottom of the bowl and then up and over, close to the surface. Turn the bowl for even distribution.
Garnish	To decorate a food or plate with small pieces of food to provide color or texture.
Grate	To rub food across a grating surface to produce small, fine particles.
Mince	To chop food into small irregular pieces.
Partially set	To chill gelatin mixtures until the consistency resembles raw egg whites.
Purée	To convert food into a liquid or paste by blending with a small amount of liquid using a blender or food processor.
Roast	To cook uncovered in the oven.
Sauté	To cook in a small amount of hot fat.
Scald	To bring food to a temperature just below boiling. Tiny bubbles will form at the edges of the pan.
Scallop	To bake food in a sauce.
Shred	To rub food on a shredder to form long, narrow pieces.
Sift	To place dry ingredients in a sifter to incorporate air and break up lumps.
Simmer	To cook food in liquid over a low heat. Bubbles will form at a slow rate and burst before reaching the surface.
Stew	To simmer slowly in small amount of liquid.
Stir	To mix food with a spoon using a circular motion.
Toss	To mix ingredients lightly by lifting and dropping them with a spoon or a spoon and fork.
Whip	To beat food lightly and rapidly to incorporate air and increase volume. Often done with a whisk.

Basic Measuring Techniques

All ingredients are not measured by the same method. To assure the best results when using a recipe, familiarize yourself and your staff with the following procedures.

Liquids. Use a clearly marked measuring cup designed for liquids. Place the cup on a level surface; do not hold it. Fill to the appropriate level. If the container is made of glass, bend down so that you are eye-level with the desired mark.

Dry Ingredients. If possible use a dry measure with exactly the capacity you wish to measure. Place the ingredients into the cup—do not pack any ingredients except brown sugar. Level off with a metal spatula.

Dried Herbs. Lightly fill measuring spoon to the top. Keep the level as close to the top as possible, but do not level with a spatula. Empty the spoon into your hand and crush with the other hand to release the flavor. (For larger amounts a small bowl and a spoon can be used.)

Solid Shortening. Pack into a dry measure using a spatula. Run spatula through shortening to make sure no air pockets remain. Level with the spatula. For margarine or butter, remember that a quarter pound stick equals ½ cup, and one-half of a stick equals ¼ cup.

Substitutions

All is not necessarily lost when a certain recipe ingredient is not available. Some substituting can be done without loss of quality if cooks are familiar with appropriate substitutions.

If the recipe calls for . . .	*You may substitute . . .*
1 C cake flour	1 C minus 2 T all-purpose flour
1 T cornstarch	2 T all-purpose flour
1 t baking powder	¼ t baking soda plus ½ C buttermilk (to replace ½ C of liquid specified)
1 package active dry yeast	1 cake compressed yeast
1 C granulated sugar	1 C packed brown sugar or 2 C sifted powdered sugar
1 C honey	1¼ C granulated sugar plus ¼ C liquid
1 C corn syrup	1 C granulated sugar plus ¼ C liquid
1 oz unsweetened chocolate	3 T unsweetened cocoa powder plus 1 T butter or margarine
1 C whipping cream, whipped	2 C whipped dessert topping
1 C buttermilk	1 T lemon juice or vinegar plus enough whole milk to make 1 C. Let stand 5 minutes before using
1 C whole milk	½ C evaporated milk plus ½ C water or 1 C reconstituted nonfat dry milk
1 C light cream	2 T butter plus 1 C minus 2 T milk
1 whole egg	2 egg yolks
1 C tomato juice	½ C tomato sauce plus ½ C water
1 clove garlic	⅛ t dried onion powder or 1 T minced, dried onion rehydrated
1 t dry mustard	1 T prepared mustard
1 t finely shredded lemon peel	½ t lemon extract

Modifying Recipes for Therapeutic Diets

Many recipes can be used for therapeutic diets either by modification of ingredients or by specific calculation into the diet. Examples of how this may be done for some diets are given below.

RESTRICTED SODIUM DIETS

Restricted sodium diets are generally planned according to level of restriction. This level must be known before planning can begin. The most common levels of restriction are 2 gms sodium and "low sodium" diets that are usually interpreted as 3 to 4 gms of sodium, depending on the diet manual used.

To modify recipes for sodium-restricted diets the sodium level listed for the recipe can be used to calculate a specific recipe into the diet. To convert milligrams of sodium to grams divide by 1000. For example, a recipe containing 500 mg of sodium contains .5 gms. If the level of sodium in the recipe is too high for this to be practical, sodium can be reduced by 1) removing the portion for restricted sodium diets before additional salt is added for seasoning; and 2) preparing the recipe as instructed but substituting low sodium products for products that contain high amounts of sodium. Examples of this include using low sodium soup instead of regular soup, or using fresh vegetables in place of the higher sodium canned variety.

RESTRICTED FAT DIETS

As is the case with restricted sodium diets, restricted fat diets must be planned according to the level of restriction.

Here again, recipes can be incorporated by planning the exact amount of fat in the diet as listed in the nutritional analysis. Other suggestions for modifying the fat content of recipes are given in section "Institutional Menus and the Dietary Guidelines for Americans."

DIABETIC DIETS

Diabetic diets are planned for a specific level of calories and may also be planned to provide exact amounts of carbohydrates, protein, and fat. The levels of the nutrients, as well as the number of calories listed in the nutritional analysis, can be used to incorporate many of the recipes in the book into diabetic diets.

The nutritional analysis can be used to convert nutrient amounts into diabetic exchanges by using the following information:

1. A bread exchange contains 15 gms of carbohydrate and 3 gms of protein.
2. A fat exchange contains 5 gms of fat.
3. An average meat exchange contains 7 gms of protein and 5 gms of fat.
4. A fruit exchange contains 15 gms of carbohydrate.
5. A vegetable exchange contains 5 gms of carbohydrate and 2 gms of protein.

Consider the following nutrient analysis:

Carbohydrates 30 gms
Protein 8 gms
Fat 10 gms

Using the information pertaining to the exchange list, the following conversion can be made:

2 bread exchanges (30 gms divided by 15 = 2)
1 meat exchange (8 gms divided by 7 = 1)
2 fat exchanges (10 gms divided by 5 = 2)

Amounts can be rounded to the nearest exchange.

In this manner many "normal" recipes can be used for diabetics. This may result in happier diabetics, as well as happier cooks, since substitutions may be minimized.

BLAND DIETS

Modern-day bland diets in no way resemble their restrictive predecessors. Individualization is the key to this diet with few foods being restricted other than those not tolerated by the specific resident.

Consult your diet manual to determine which foods, if any, to restrict.

PART II *Recipes*

CHAPTER 4 *Breads, Soups, and Salads*

ANGEL BISCUITS

CATEGORY: Bread   PORTION: 2" biscuit

INGREDIENTS	10	20	30	40	50	60	70	80	90	100
Dry Yeast	1½ t	2½ t	3½ t	4½ t	2 T	2½ T	3 T	3½ T	4 T	4½ T
Water, lukewarm	1 T	1½ T	2 T	3 T	4 T	4½ T	5 T	6 T	7 T	8 T
Buttermilk	6 oz	12 oz	1 pt 4 oz	1 pt 8 oz	1 qt	1 qt 6 oz	1 qt 12 oz	1 qt	1 qt 24 oz	2 qt
Flour	2 C	4 C	6 C	8 C	10 C	12 C	4 lb	4 lb 8 oz	5 lb	6 lb
Sugar	1 T	1 oz	2 oz	3 oz	4 oz	4 oz	6 oz	7 oz	7 oz	8 oz
Baking Powder	1½ t	2½ t	3½ t	4 t	2 T	2 T	2½ T	3 T	3½ T	4 T
Baking Soda	¼ t	½ t	¾ t	1 t	1 t	1¼ t	1½ t	1¾ t	2 t	2 t
Salt	½ t	¾ t	1¼ t	1½ t	2 t	2¼ t	2½ t	3 t	3¼ t	3½ t
Shortening	4 oz	6 oz	8 oz	12 oz	1 lb	1 lb 4 oz	1 lb 6 oz	1 lb 8 oz	1 lb 12 oz	2 lb

Nutrient Analysis per serving

Protein:	3 g
Carbohydrate:	20 g
Fat:	9 g
Sodium:	188 mg
Kilocalories:	171

Procedure

1. Dissolve yeast in lukewarm water. Stir well and add lukewarm buttermilk.
2. Sift together the flour, sugar, baking powder, soda, and salt.
3. Cut in shortening to the flour mixture and mix until spongy. Turn out onto floured board and add more flour if needed to handle well.
4. Let dough rest for 5 minutes.
5. Place dough in greased bowl and refrigerate for one hour.
6. Roll out dough, cut into biscuits. Dip in melted margarine and let rise until doubled.
7. Bake at 400°F until lightly browned, approximately 12–15 minutes.

APPLE CORN MUFFINS

CATEGORY: Bread   PORTION: 1 muffin

INGREDIENTS	10	20	30	40	50	60	70	80	90	100
Corn Muffin Mix	8 oz	1 lb 2 oz	1 lb 12 oz	2 lb 4 oz	2 lb 12 oz	3 lb 6 oz	4 lb	4 lb 8 oz	5 lb	5 lb 8 oz
Water	6 oz	12 oz	1 lb 2 oz	1 lb 8 oz	1 lb 12 oz	2 lb 2 oz	2 lb 8 oz	2 lb 24 oz	3 lb 2 oz	3 lb 8 oz
Apples, chopped (canned or fresh)	⅓ C	⅔ C	1 C	1⅓ C	1⅔ C	2 C	2⅓ C	2⅔ C	3 C	3⅓ C

Nutrient Analysis per serving

Protein:	2 g
Carbohydrate:	16 g
Fat:	5 g
Sodium:	229 mg
Kilocalories:	120

Procedure

1. Follow package directions to complete the batter. Add chopped apples and mix well.
2. Pour into well greased and floured or paper-lined cupcake pans. Sprinkle tops lightly with cinnamon sugar.
3. Bake in 425°F oven for 15 minutes.

CREAM CHEESE MUFFINS

CATEGORY: Bread   PORTION: 1 muffin

INGREDIENTS	10	20	30	40	50	60	70	80	90	100
Baking Mix	2½ C	5 C	7½ C	10 C	12 C	14½ C	17 C	19 C	22 C	24 C
Sugar	4 oz	8 oz	12 oz	1 lb	1 lb 4 oz	1 lb 8 oz	1 lb 12 oz	2 lb	2 lb 4 oz	2 lb 8 oz
Nutmeg	Pinch	⅛ t	¼ t	½ t	¾ t	1 t	1⅛ t	1¼ t	1½ t	1½ t
Cinnamon	¼ t	½ t	¾ t	1 t	1½ t	1¾ t	2 t	2¼ t	2½ t	3 t
Eggs	2 oz	3 oz	4 oz	5 oz	6 oz	8 oz	9 oz	10 oz	11 oz	12 oz
Water	¾ C	1½ C	2¼ C	3 C	3¾ C	4½ C	5¼ C	6 C	6¾ C	7½ C
Raisins	⅓ C	⅔ C	1 C	1⅓ C	1½ C	1¾ C	2 C	2¼ C	2½ C	3 C
Cream Cheese	4 oz	8 oz	12 oz	1 lb	1 lb 8 oz	1 lb 12 oz	2 lb	2 lb 4 oz	2 lb 8 oz	3 lb
Eggs	2 oz	3 oz	4 oz	5 oz	6 oz	8 oz	9 oz	10 oz	11 oz	12 oz
Sugar	2 oz	3 oz	4 oz	5 oz	6 oz	8 oz	9 oz	10 oz	11 oz	12 oz

Nutrient Analysis per serving

Protein:	4 g
Carbohydrate:	39 g
Fat:	9 g
Sodium:	400 mg
Kilocalories:	254

Procedure

1. Combine first four ingredients. Blend. Add eggs and water, mixing just until moistened. Stir in raisins.
2. In separate bowl, combine softened cream cheese, sugar, and eggs, mixing until well blended. Gently fold cream cheese mixture into batter.
3. Spoon batter into greased muffin tins, filling ⅔ full. Bake at 350°F for about 25 minutes.

PECAN COFFEE CAKE

INGREDIENTS	10	20	30	40	50	60	70	80	90	100
Biscuit Mix	12 oz	1 lb 8 oz	2 lb	2 lb 8 oz	3 lb 4 oz	4 lb	4 lb 8 oz	5 lb	6 lb	7 lb 8 oz
Sugar	6 oz	12 oz	1 lb 2 oz	1 lb 8 oz	2 lb	2 lb 6 oz	2 lb 12 oz	3 lb 2 oz	3 lb 10 oz	4 lb
Milk	6 oz	12 oz	1 pt	1 pt 8 oz	1 qt	1 qt 6 oz	1 qt 12 oz	1 qt 16 oz	1 qt 24 oz	2 qt
Egg	1	2	3	4	5	6	7	8	9	10
Margarine	3 T	3 oz	4 oz	6 oz	8 oz	10 oz	12 oz	13 oz	14 oz	1 lb
Vanilla	1 t	2 t	3 t	4 t	5 t	6 t	7 t	8 t	9 t	10 t
TOPPING:										
Brown Sugar	4 oz	8 oz	12 oz	1 lb	1 lb 4 oz	1 lb 8 oz	1 lb 12 oz	2 lb	2 lb 4 oz	2.5 lb
Pecan Halves	4 oz	8 oz	12 oz	1 lb	1 lb 4 oz	1 lb 8 oz	1 lb 12 oz	2 lb	2 lb 4 oz	2.5 lb
Margarine, soft	2 oz	3 oz	4 oz	5 oz	6 oz	7 oz	8 oz	9 oz	10 oz	12 oz
Light Cream	1 T	2 T	3 T	4 T	5 T	6 T	7 T	8 T	9 T	10 T

Nutrient Analysis per serving

Protein:	4 g
Carbohydrate:	51 g
Fat:	21 g
Sodium:	480 mg
Kilocalories:	396

Procedure

1. Combine biscuit mix, sugar, half of the milk, egg, margarine, and vanilla.
2. Beat at medium speed for one minute.
3. Add remaining milk and beat ½ minute.
4. Pour into greased and floured rectangular baking pan. Bake in 350°F oven for 35 to 40 minutes.
5. Mix all topping ingredients and spread over baked cakes. Broil about 4 inches from heat until bubbly.

PRUNE COFFEE CAKE

CATEGORY: *Bread*   PORTION: *2½" square*

INGREDIENTS	10	20	30	40	50	60	70	80	90	100
Butter or Margarine	3½ t	4½ t	5 t	6½ t	7 t	8 t	9 t	10 t	11 t	12 t
Sugar	¾ C	1½ C	2¼ C	3 C	4 C	4¾ C	5½ C	6¼ C	7 C	8 C
Eggs	2	3	5	6	8	10	11	13	14	16
Cooked, pitted prunes, drained	¾ C	1½ C	2¼ C	3 C	3¾ C	4½ C	5¼ C	6 C	6¾ C	7½ C
TOPPING										
Butter or Margarine	1½ t	1 T	1½ T	2 T	3 T	3½ T	4 T	4½ T	5 T	6 T
Sugar	1½ t	1 T	1½ T	2 T	3 T	3½ T	4 T	4½ T	5 T	6 T
Cinnamon	1½ t	1 T	1½ T	2 T	3 T	3½ T	4 T	4½ T	5 T	6 T
Flour	1 T	1 oz	2 oz	3 oz	4 oz	5 oz	6 oz	7 oz	8 oz	9 oz

Nutrient Analysis per serving

Protein: 1 g
Carbohydrate: 21 g
Fat: 2 g
Sodium: 28 mg
Kilocalories: 105

Procedure

1. Spread batter in greased 12″ × 20″ baking pan.
2. Sprinkle with topping.
3. Bake at 350°F for 35 to 40 minutes. Serve warm with butter or margarine.

PUMPKIN MUFFINS

CATEGORY: Bread   PORTION: 1

INGREDIENTS	10	20	30	40	50	60	70	80	90	100
Baking Mix, all-purpose	8 oz	1 lb 4 oz	2 lb	2 lb 8 oz	3 lb 4 oz	4 lb	4 lb 8 oz	5 lb 4 oz	6 lb	6 lb 8 oz
Light Brown Sugar	2 oz	4 oz	8 oz	10 oz	12 oz	1 lb	1 lb 2 oz	1 lb 4 oz	1 lb 8 oz	1 lb 12 oz
Cinnamon	¼ t	½ t	1 t	1¼ t	1½ t	2 t	2¼ t	2½ t	3 t	3¼ t
Nutmeg	¼ t	½ t	1 t	1¼ t	1½ t	2 t	2¼ t	2½ t	3 t	3¼ t
Molasses	2 oz	4 oz	6 oz	8 oz	10 oz	12 oz	14 oz	1 pt	1 pt 2 oz	1 pt 4 oz
Pumpkin, mashed	6 oz	12 oz	1 lb	1 lb 6 oz	1 lb 12 oz	2 lb	2 lb 6 oz	2 lb 12 oz	3 lb	3 lb 6 oz
Water	4 oz	8 oz	12 oz	1 pt	1 pt 4 oz	1 pt 8 oz	1 pt 12 oz	2 pt	2 pt 4 oz	2 pt 8 oz
Eggs	1	3	4	6	7	8	10	11	13	14

Nutrient Analysis per serving

Protein:	2 g
Carbohydrate:	26 g
Fat:	4 g
Sodium:	310 mg
Kilocalories:	150

Procedure

1. Combine first four ingredients. Blend. Add molasses, pumpkin, water, and eggs. Mix until just moistened.
2. Spoon batter into greased muffin tins, filling ⅔ full.
3. Bake at 350°F for 30 minutes or until golden brown.

PUMPKIN NUT BREAD

CATEGORY: Bread   PORTION: 1, 2" square

INGREDIENTS	10	20	30	40	50	60	70	80	90	100
Basic Muffin Mix	1 lb	2 lb	3 lb	4 lb	5 lb	6 lb	7 lb	8 lb	9 lb	10 lb
Water	6 oz	12 oz	1 pt 2 oz	1 pt 8 oz	1 qt	1 qt 6 oz	1 qt 12 oz	1 qt 18 oz	1 qt 24 oz	2 qt
Pumpkin, canned	2 oz	3 oz	4 oz	6 oz	8 oz	10 oz	11 oz	12 oz	14 oz	1 lb
Nuts, finely chopped	¼ C	⅓ C	½ C	¾ C	1 C	1¼ C	1⅓ C	1½ C	1¾ C	2 C
Baking Soda	⅛ t	¼ t	½ t	¾ t	1 t	1⅛ t	1¼ t	1½ t	1⅓ t	2 t
Sugar	2 oz	3 oz	4 oz	6 oz	8 oz	10 oz	11 oz	12 oz	14 oz	1 lb

Nutrient Analysis per serving

Protein:	3 g
Carbohydrate:	32 g
Fat:	7 g
Sodium:	487 mg
Kilocalories:	203

Procedure

1. Place mix in mixing bowl. Add half of the water. Mix for two minutes.
2. Add all remaining ingredients and mix two more minutes.
3. Pour into greased and floured loaf pans ⅔ full.
4. Bake 40 to 45 minutes at 375°F.
5. Cool before slicing.

40   Recipes

WHOLE WHEAT MUFFINS

CATEGORY: Bread   PORTION: 1

INGREDIENTS	10	20	30	40	50	60	70	80	90	100
Flour, all-purpose	12 oz	1 lb 8 oz	2 lb 6 oz	3 lb	4 lb	4 lb 12 oz	5 lb 8 oz	6 lb 6 oz	7 lb	8 lb
Whole Wheat Flour	2 oz	4 oz	8 oz	12 oz	1 lb	1 lb 2 oz	1 lb 4 oz	1 lb 8 oz	1 lb 12 oz	2 lb
Nonfat Dry Milk	1 oz	2 oz	3 oz	4 oz	5 oz	6 oz	7 oz	8 oz	9 oz	10 oz
Baking Powder	1 oz	2 oz	3 oz	4 oz	5 oz	6 oz	7 oz	8 oz	9 oz	10 oz
Salt	1½ t	2½ t	3 t	3½ t	4 t	4½ t	5 t	5½ t	6 t	6½ t
Shortening	2 oz	4 oz	8 oz	12 oz	1 lb	1 lb 2 oz	1 lb 4 oz	1 lb 8 oz	1 lb 12 oz	2 lb

Nutrient Analysis per serving

Protein: 5 g
Carbohydrate: 32 g
Fat: 6 g
Sodium: 503 mg
Kilocalories: 203

Procedure

1. Blend dry ingredients in mixer on low speed. Cut in shortening and butter.
2. Add eggs. Mix well, adding milk slowly.
3. Using #16 scoop (¼ cup), portion into greased muffin pans.
4. Bake 20 minutes at 400°F.

CHICKEN NOODLE SOUP

CATEGORY: *Soup*   PORTION: *8 oz*

INGREDIENTS	10	20	30	40	50	60	70	80	90	100
Chicken, fresh, cut up	3 lb	6 lb	9 lb	12 lb	15 lb	18 lb	21 lb	24 lb	27 lb	30 lb
Water	1 qt 8 oz	2 qt 16 oz	3 qt 24 oz	5 qt	6 qt 8 oz	7 qt 16 oz	8 qt 24 oz	10 qt	11 qt 8 oz	12 qt 16 oz
Carrots, fresh, cut into slices	2½ C	5 C	7½ C	10 C	12½ C	15 C	17½ C	20 C	22½ C	25 C
Celery, fresh, cut into slices	2½ C	5 C	7½ C	10 C	12½ C	15 C	17½ C	20 C	22½ C	25 C
Salt	2½ t	1½ T	2½ T	3 T	4 T	5 T	6 T	7 T	8 T	9 T
Monosodium Glutamate	2½ t	1½ T	2½ T	3 T	4 T	5 T	6 T	7 T	8 T	9 T
Chicken Soup Base	2½ t	1½ T	2½ T	3 T	4 T	5 T	6 T	7 T	8 T	9 T
Egg Noodles, uncooked	1½ C	2½ C	4 C	5 C	7 C	8 C	9 C	10 C	12 C	13 C

Nutrient Analysis per serving

Protein:	14 g
Carbohydrate:	11 g
Fat:	21 g
Sodium:	846 mg
Kilocalories:	289

Procedure

1. Heat all ingredients except noodles to boiling in large pot. Reduce heat and simmer until chicken is done (about 1 hour). Skim fat if necessary.
2. Cook noodles according to package directions. Drain.
3. Remove chicken from bones and skin. Cut into 1″ pieces.
4. Add chicken and cooked noodles to broth and reheat.

CREAM OF POTATO SOUP

CATEGORY: *Soup*   PORTION: *1, 6 oz ladle*

INGREDIENTS	10	20	30	40	50	60	70	80	90	100
Potatoes, cooked, diced	2 lb 8 oz	5 lb	7 lb	9 lb 8 oz	12 lb	14 lb 8 oz	17 lb	19 lb	21 lb 8 oz	24 lb
Margarine	2 oz	4 oz	8 oz	10 oz	12 oz	14 oz	1 lb	1 lb 2 oz	1 lb 4 oz	1 lb 8 oz
Flour	1 oz	2 oz	3 oz	4 oz	6 oz	7 oz	8 oz	10 oz	11 oz	12 oz
Salt	1 t	2 t	3 t	4 t	4½ t	5 t	5½ t	6 t	6½ t	7 t
White Pepper	Pinch	Dash	⅛ t	¼ t	½ t	¾ t	¾ t	1 t	1 t	1¼ t
Milk, hot	1 qt 24 oz	3 qt 16 oz	1 gal 3 pt	1 gal 3 qt	2 gal 1 qt	2 gal 2 qt	2 gal 3 qt	3 gal 3 pt	4 gal	4 gal 2 qt
Onion, chopped	1 oz	2 oz	4 oz	5 oz	6 oz	7 oz	8 oz	9 oz	10 oz	11 oz

Nutrient Analysis per serving

Protein:	8 g
Carbohydrate:	33 g
Fat:	8 g
Sodium:	262 mg
Kilocalories:	235

Procedure

1. Melt margarine. Add flour, salt, white pepper, and *hot* milk.
2. Add cooked vegetables and serve.

CREAM OF VEGETABLE SOUP

CATEGORY: *Soup*   PORTION: *8 oz*

INGREDIENTS	10	20	30	40	50	60	70	80	90	100
Mixed vegetables, frozen	1 lb	2 lb	3 lb	4 lb	5 lb	6 lb	7 lb	8 lb	9 lb	10 lb
Pimientos, diced	1 oz	2 oz	3 oz	4 oz	5 oz	6 oz	7 oz	8 oz	8 oz	10 oz
Parsley Flakes	1 t	2 t	1 T	1 T	1½ T	1½ T	2 T	2 T	3 T	3 T
Canned Cream of Chicken Soup, undiluted	1 qt	2 qt	3 qt	1 gal	1 gal 1 qt	1 gal 2 qt	1 gal 3 qt	2 gal	2 gal 1 qt	2 gal 2 qt
Vegetable Liquid, plus water	1 qt	2 qt	3 qt	1 gal	1 gal 1 qt	1 gal 2 qt	1 gal 3 qt	2 gal	2 gal 1 qt	2 gal 2 qt

Nutrient Analysis per serving

Protein:	4 g
Carbohydrate:	13 g
Fat:	5 g
Sodium:	805 mg
Kilocalories:	121

Procedure

1. Cook mixed vegetables in boiling water until just tender, about 15 minutes. Drain and reserve liquid.
2. Add pimientos and parsley to drained vegetables.
3. Combine soup and vegetable liquid in large pot; add vegetable mixture.
4. Heat to boiling.

Note: Recipe may be made with milk instead of water.

ITALIAN TOMATO SOUP

INGREDIENTS	10	20	30	40	50	60	70	80	90	100
Zucchini	8 oz	1 lb	1 lb 8 oz	2 lb	2 lb 8 oz	3 lb	3 lb 8 oz	4 lb	4 lb 8 oz	5 lb
Salt	1 t	2 t	3 t	4 t	5 t	6 t	7 t	8 t	9 t	10 t
Oregano, crushed	1 t	2 t	1 T	1 T 1 t	1 T 2 t	2 T	2 T 1 t	2 T 2 t	3 T	3 T 1 t
Garlic, granulated	dash	¼ t	½ t	¾ t	1 t	1¼ t	1½ t	1¾ t	2 t	2¼ t
Water, boiling	1 qt	2 qt	3 qt	1 gal	1 gal 1 qt	1 gal 2 qt	1 gal 3 qt	2 gal	2 gal 1 qt	2 gal 2 qt
Tomato Soup, condensed	1 qt	2 qt	3 qt	1 gal	1 gal 1 qt	1 gal 2 qt	1 gal 3 qt	2 gal	2 gal 1 qt	2 gal 2 qt
Macaroni, uncooked	4 oz	8 oz	12 oz	1 lb 2 oz	1 lb 4 oz	1 lb 8 oz	1 lb 12 oz	2 lb 4 oz	2 lb 6 oz	2 lb 8 oz

Nutrient Analysis per serving

Protein:	2 g
Carbohydrate:	20 g
Fat:	1 g
Sodium:	816 mg
Kilocalories:	104

Procedure

1. Add zucchini, salt, oregano, and garlic to boiling water. Cover; cook only until zucchini is crisp-tender.
2. Gently stir in soup. Add cooked macaroni. Heat to a boil; simmer a few minutes to blend flavors.

NAVY BEAN SOUP

CATEGORY: *Soup*   PORTION: *1 C*

INGREDIENTS	10	20	30	40	50	60	70	80	90	100
Navy Beans	8 oz	1 lb	1 lb 8 oz	2 lb 4 oz	3 lb	3 lb 8 oz	4 lb	4 lb 8 oz	5 lb 4 oz	6 lb
Water, boiling	1 qt 4 oz	2 qt 12 oz	3 qt 16 oz	5 qt	6 qt	8 qt	8 qt 16 oz	10 qt	10 qt 16 oz	12 qt
Ham Shank	1 lb	2 lb	3 lb	4 lb	5 lb	6 lb	7 lb	8 lb	9 lb	10 lb
Onion, chopped	1 T	1 oz	2 oz	3 oz	4 oz	4½ oz	5 oz	6 oz	7 oz	8 oz
Celery, chopped	2 oz	3 oz	4 oz	6 oz	8 oz	10 oz	11 oz	12 oz	14 oz	1 lb

Nutrient Analysis per serving

Protein:	11 g
Carbohydrate:	11 g
Fat:	10 g
Sodium:	573 mg
Kilocalories:	173

Procedure

1. Wash beans. Add boiling water. Cover and let stand one hour or longer.
2. Add ham shank and simmer until beans are cooked.
3. Remove ham from bones, chop, and save to add later.
4. Add onion, celery, and additional water as needed. Cook 30 minutes and add chopped ham.

TOMATO-CELERY SOUP

INGREDIENTS	10	20	30	40	50	60	70	80	90	100
Onion, chopped	1	2	3	4	5	6	7	8	9	10
Margarine	1 oz	2 oz	3 oz	4 oz	5 oz	6 oz	7 oz	8 oz	9 oz	10 oz
Tomato Soup, canned	8 oz	1 pt 4 oz	1 qt	1 qt 8 oz	1 qt 16 oz	2 qt	2 qt 8 oz	2 qt 16 oz	3 qt	3 qt 8 oz
Parsley, minced	1 t	2 t	3 t	4 t	5 t	6 t	7 t	8 t	9 t	10 t
Pepper	⅛ t	¼ t	⅓ t	½ t	⅔ t	¾ t	¾ t	1 t	1⅛ t	1¼ t
Celery, chopped	½ C	1 C	1½ C	2 C	2½ C	3 C	3½ C	4 C	4½ C	5 C
Lemon Juice	1 T	1½ T	2 T	3 T	4 T	5 T	5½ T	6 T	7 T	8 T
Sugar	1 t	2 t	3 t	4 t	5 t	6 t	7 t	8 t	9 t	10 t
Salt	¼ t	½ t	¾ t	1 t	1¼ t	1½ t	1¾ t	2 t	2¼ t	2½ t
Water	10½ oz	1 pt 4 oz	2 pt	2 pt 8 oz	1 qt 20 oz	2 qt	2 qt 8 oz	2 qt 16 oz	3 qt	3 qt 8 oz

Nutrient Analysis per serving

Protein:	1 g
Carbohydrate:	5 g
Fat:	3 g
Sodium:	292 mg
Kilocalories:	46

Procedure

1. Sauté onion and celery in margarine; do not brown.
2. Add tomato soup, water, parsley, lemon juice, sugar, salt, and pepper. Simmer 5 minutes. Celery will remain crisp.
3. Top with unsweetened whipped cream and chopped parsley.

BANANA SALAD

CATEGORY: *Salad*   PORTION: ½ C, #8 dipper

INGREDIENTS	10	20	30	40	50	60	70	80	90	100
Salad Dressing	4 oz	6 oz	8 oz	12 oz	1 pt	1 pt 4 oz	1 pt 6 oz	1 pt 8 oz	1 pt 12 oz	1 qt
Peanut Butter	½ C	¾ C	1¼ C	1½ C	2 C	2½ C	2¾ C	3¼ C	3½ C	4 C
Milk	¼ C	½ C	¾ C	1 C	1½ C	1¾ C	2 C	2¼ C	2½ C	3 C
Honey	1½ T	3 T	¼ C	⅓ C	½ C	½ C	⅔ C	¾ C	¾ C	1 C
Corn Flakes, crushed	4 oz	8 oz	12 oz	1 lb	1 lb 8 oz	1 lb 12 oz	2 lb	2 lb 2 oz	2 lb 8 oz	2 lb 16 oz
Bananas	2 lb 8 oz	5 lb	7 lb 8 oz	10 lb	12 lb 8 oz	15 lb	17 lb 8 oz	20 lb	22 lb 8 oz	25 lb

Nutrient Analysis per serving

Protein: 7 g
Carbohydrate: 50 g
Fat: 16 g
Sodium: 268 mg
Kilocalories: 353

Procedure

1. Slice bananas and soak in orange juice in order to avoid browning. Set aside.
2. Mix salad dressing, honey, and peanut butter together. Blend to a smooth consistency.
3. Add milk to blended mixture and stir.
4. Drain bananas well. Fold bananas into dressing mixture.
5. Gently add finely crushed corn flakes to mixture.
6. Place #8 scoop on lettuce leaf.

CALICO MACARONI SALAD

INGREDIENTS	10	20	30	40	50	60	70	80	90	100
Macaroni	8 oz	1 lb	1 lb 8 oz	2 lb	2 lb 8 oz	3 lb	3 lb 8 oz	4 lb	4 lb 8 oz	5 lb
Mixed Vegetables, frozen	1 lb	2 lb	3 lb	4 lb	5 lb	6 lb	7 lb	8 lb	9 lb	10 lb
Cheddar Cheese, diced	6 oz	12 oz	1 lb 2 oz	1 lb 8 oz	2 lb	2 lb 6 oz	2 lb 12 oz	3 lb 2 oz	3 lb 8 oz	4 lb
Mayonnaise	6 oz	12 oz	1 pt 2 oz	1 pt 10 oz	1 qt	1 qt 6 oz	1 qt 12 oz	1 qt 16 oz	1 qt 24 oz	2 qt
Onion Salt	½ t	1 t	2 t	3 t	4 t	4½ t	5 t	6 t	7 t	8 t
Pepper	⅛ t	¼ t	½ t	¾ t	1 t	1⅛ t	1¼ t	1½ t	1¾ t	2 t

Nutrient Analysis per serving

Protein:	6 g
Carbohydrate:	14 g
Fat:	19 g
Sodium:	272 mg
Kilocalories:	256

Procedure

1. Cook macaroni. Drain and chill.
2. Cook the frozen vegetables. Drain and chill.
3. Add cheese, mayonnaise, onion salt, and pepper.
4. Chill. Serve with #12 dipper.

CARRIFRUIT SALAD

CATEGORY: *Salad*   PORTION: ½ C, #8 dipper

INGREDIENTS	10	20	30	40	50	60	70	80	90	100
Carrots, fresh, shredded	2 lb	4 lb	6 lb	7 lb	8 lb	10 lb	12 lb	14 lb	15 lb	16 lb
Pineapple Tidbits, drained	12 oz	24 oz	1 qt 6 oz	1 qt 16 oz	2 qt	2 qt 12 oz	2 qt 24 oz	3 qt 6 oz	3 qt 16 oz	3 qt 24 oz
Coconut, flaked	8 oz	1 lb	1 lb 8 oz	2 lb	2 lb 8 oz	3 lb	3 lb 8 oz	4 lb	4 lb 8 oz	5 lb
Salt	Pinch	⅛ t	¼ t	½ t	¾ t	¾ t	1 t	1 t	1¼ t	1½ t
Salad Dressing, prepared	8 oz	1 pt	1 pt 8 oz	1 qt	1 qt 12 oz	1 qt 16 oz	1 qt 24 oz	2 qt	2 qt 12 oz	2 qt 16 oz

Nutrient Analysis per serving

Protein:	2 g
Carbohydrate:	20 g
Fat:	21 g
Sodium:	206 mg
Kilocalories:	267

Procedure

1. Mix all ingredients.
2. Toss lightly.

COLORFUL FRUIT AND MELON SALAD

CATEGORY: Salad   PORTION: ½ C, #8 dipper

INGREDIENTS	10	20	30	40	50	60	70	80	90	100
Vanilla	½ T	¾ T	1 T	1½ T	2 T	2½ T	2¾ T	3 T	3½ T	4 T
Whipped Cream	½ C	1 C	1½ C	2 C	2½ C	3 C	3½ C	4 C	4½ C	5 C
Sugar	2 T	¼ C	⅓ C	½ C	⅔ C	¾ C	¾ C	1 C	1¼ C	1⅓ C
Cantaloupe	3	5	8	10	13	16	18	21	23	26
Apples, diced	1 lb 8 oz	3 lb 4 oz	4 lb 12 oz	6 lb 8 oz	8 lb	9 lb 8 oz	11 lb 4 oz	12 lb 12 oz	14 lb 8 oz	16 lb
Bananas, sliced	12 oz	1 lb 8 oz	2 lb 4 oz	3 lb	3 lb 12 oz	4 lb 8 oz	5 lb 4 oz	6 lb	6 lb 12 oz	7 lb 8 oz
Grapes	12 oz	1 lb 8 oz	2 lb 8 oz	3 lb 4 oz	4 lb 2 oz	5 lb	5 lb 12 oz	6 lb 8 oz	7 lb 6 oz	8 lb 6 oz
Maraschino Cherries	10	20	30	40	50	60	70	80	90	100

Nutrient Analysis per serving

Protein:	3 g
Carbohydrate:	45 g
Fat:	5 g
Sodium:	20 mg
Kilocalories:	218

Procedure

1. Whip cream with vanilla and sugar until stiff peaks form.
2. Quarter and clean the cantaloupe.
3. Fold cream into sliced fruit.
4. Portion onto melon quarter with #12 scoop.
5. Garnish each melon slice with cherry.

CRANBERRY BANANA DELIGHT SALAD

CATEGORY: Salad   *PORTION: 1/3 C, # 12 dipper*

INGREDIENTS	10	20	30	40	50	60	70	80	90	100
Strawberry Gelatin	4 oz	8 oz	12 oz	1 lb	1 lb 8 oz	1 lb 12 oz	2 lb	2 lb 2 oz	2 lb 8 oz	3 lb
Whole Cranberry Sauce	8 oz	1 lb	1 lb 8 oz	2 lb 6 oz	3 lb	3 lb 8 oz	4 lb	4 lb 8 oz	5 lb 6 oz	6 lb
Water, hot	1 pt	1 qt	1 qt 16 oz	2 qt	2 qt 16 oz	3 qt	3 qt 16 oz	1 gal	1 gal 16 oz	5 qt
Apples, diced	6 oz	12 oz	1 lb 2 oz	1 lb 8 oz	2 lb	2 lb 6 oz	2 lb 12 oz	3 lb 2 oz	3 lb 8 oz	4 lb
Bananas, sliced	8 oz	1 lb	1 lb 8 oz	2 lb 6 oz	3 lb	3 lb 8 oz	4 lb	4 lb 8 oz	5 lb 6 oz	6 lb

Nutrient Analysis per serving

Protein:	2 g
Carbohydrate:	37 g
Fat:	0 g
Sodium:	155 mg
Kilocalories:	85

Procedure

1. Dissolve gelatin and cranberry sauce in hot water. Place in refrigerator until partially congealed.
2. Fold in apples and bananas. Chill until set.
3. Serve on crisp lettuce leaf and top with whipped cream.

CREAMY CUCUMBER SALAD

CATEGORY: *Salad*   PORTION: *⅓ C, # 12 scoop*

INGREDIENTS	10	20	30	40	50	60	70	80	90	100
Cucumbers	12 oz	1 lb 8 oz	2 lb 8 oz	3 lb 6 oz	4 lb 4 oz	5 lb	5 lb 12 oz	6 lb 12 oz	7 lb 12 oz	8 lb 8 oz
Onions	2 oz	4 oz	6 oz	8 oz	10 oz	12 oz	14 oz	1 lb	1 lb 2 oz	1 lb 4 oz
Sour Cream	4 oz	8 oz	14 oz	1 lb 4 oz	1 lb 8 oz	1 lb 12 oz	2 lb	2 lb 8 oz	2 lb 12 oz	1 qt 16 oz
Mayonnaise	4 oz	8 oz	14 oz	1 lb 4 oz	1 lb 8 oz	1 lb 12 oz	2 lb	2 lb 8 oz	2 lb 12 oz	1 qt 16 oz
Salt	¼ t	½ t	1 t	1¼ t	1½ t	1¾ t	2 t	2½ t	2¾ t	3 t
Sugar	½ T	1 T	1½ T	2 T	2½ T	3 T	3½ T	4 T	4½ T	5 T
Vinegar	2 oz	3 oz	4 oz	5 oz	6 oz	8 oz	10 oz	11 oz	12 oz	14 oz

Nutrient Analysis per serving

Protein:	0 g
Carbohydrate:	2 g
Fat:	13 g
Sodium:	172 mg
Kilocalories:	135

Procedure

1. Cut cucumbers and onions in thin slices.
2. Blend rest of ingredients to form a thin cream dressing.
3. Pour over cucumbers and onions.
4. Mix lightly and chill.

CRUNCHY GARDEN SLAW

CATEGORY: Salad   PORTION: ½ C, #8 dipper

INGREDIENTS	10	20	30	40	50	60	70	80	90	100
Cabbage, shredded	1 qt 8 oz	2 qt 16 oz	3 qt 16 oz	4 qt 24 oz	6 qt	7 qt 8 oz	8 qt 16 oz	9 qt 16 oz	10 qt 24 oz	12 qt
Celery, thinly sliced	1¼ C	2½ C	3¾ C	5 C	6¼ C	7½ C	8¾ C	10 C	11¼ C	13 C
Cucumber, chopped	1¼ C	2½ C	3¾ C	5 C	6¼ C	7½ C	8¾ C	10 C	10¼ C	13 C
Green Pepper, chopped	½ C	1 C	1½ C	2 C	3 C	3½ C	4 C	4½ C	5 C	6 C
Salad Dressing	4 oz	8 oz	12 oz	1 pt	1 pt 4 oz	1 pt 12 oz	1 qt	1 qt 4 oz	1 qt 8 oz	1 qt 16 oz
Vinegar	2 T	¼ C	⅓ C	½ C	¾ C	¾ C	1 C	1¼ C	1⅓ C	1½ C
Mustard, prepared	1¼ t	2½ t	3½ t	4¾ t	2 T	2½ T	3 T	3½ T	4 T	4½ T
Sugar	¾ t	1½ t	2¼ t	3 t	3½ t	4¼ t	5 t	5¾ t	6½ t	7 t
Paprika	¼ t	½ t	¾ t	1 t	1½ t	1¾ t	2 t	2¼ t	2½ t	3 t
Lemon Juice	1 T	2 T	3 T	4 T	5 T	6 T	7 T	8 T	9 T	10 T

Nutrient Analysis per serving

Protein:	1 g
Carbohydrate:	8 g
Fat:	9 g
Sodium:	95 mg
Kilocalories:	112

Procedure

1. Combine cabbage, celery, cucumber, and green pepper.
2. Stir together salad dressing, vinegar, mustard, sugar, salt, paprika, and lemon juice.
3. Pour salad dressing mixture over vegetables. Toss to coat vegetables.
4. Cover and chill. Garnish with chopped parsley.

EMERALD ISLE SALAD

CATEGORY: *Salad*   PORTION: *2" × 2" square*

INGREDIENTS	10	20	30	40	50	60	70	80	90	100
Lime Jello	4 oz	8 oz	12 oz	1 lb	1 lb 4 oz	1 lb 8 oz	1 lb 12 oz	2 lb	2 lb 4 oz	2 lb 8 oz
Water, boiling	8 oz	1 pt	1 pt 8 oz	1 qt 6 oz	1 qt 16 oz	1 qt 24 oz	2 qt	2 qt 8 oz	2 qt 24 oz	3 qt
Pineapple crushed, undrained	1 pt	1 qt	1 qt 16 oz	2 qt	2 qt 16 oz	3 qt	3 qt 16 oz	4 oz	4 qt 16 oz	5 qt 8 oz
Lemon Juice	1 T	2 T	3 T	4 T	5 T	6 T	7 T	8 T	9 T	10 T
Sugar	1 oz	2 oz	4 oz	5 oz	8 oz	9 oz	10 oz	12 oz	14 oz	1 lb
Marshmallows, mini	1 C	2 C	3 C	4 C	5 C	6 C	7 C	8 C	9 C	10 C
Cottage Cheese	1 C	2 C	3 C	4 C	5 C	6 C	7 C	8 C	9 C	10 C
Whipped Cream	2 oz	6 oz	8 oz	12 oz	1 pt	1 pt 2 oz	1 pt 6 oz	1 pt 8 oz	1 pt 12 oz	1 qt
Salt	¼ t	½ t	¾ t	1 t	1½ t	1¾ t	2 t	2¼ t	2½ t	3 t

Nutrient Analysis per serving

Protein:	3 g
Carbohydrate:	17 g
Fat:	3 g
Sodium:	151 mg
Kilocalories:	102

Procedure

1. Dissolve jello in boiling water.
2. Add sugar, marshmallows, pineapple, lemon juice, salt, and cottage cheese. Chill.
3. Fold in whipped cream.
4. Pour into rectangular baking pan or steamtable pans. Chill and cut into 2" × 2" squares.

FRESH FRUIT CUP

CATEGORY: *Salad*   PORTION: *5 oz*

INGREDIENTS	10	20	30	40	50	60	70	80	90	100
Grapefruit Sections	12 oz	1 pt 8 oz	1 qt 6 oz	1 qt 16 oz	2 qt	2 qt 12 oz	2 qt 24 oz	3 qt 6 oz	3 qt 16 oz	4 qt
Orange Sections	12 oz	1 pt 8 oz	1 qt 6 oz	1 qt 16 oz	2 qt	2 qt 12 oz	2 qt 24 oz	3 qt 6 oz	3 qt 16 oz	4 qt
Pineapple, diced	12 oz	1 pt 8 oz	1 qt 6 oz	1 qt 16 oz	2 qt	2 qt 12 oz	2 qt 24 oz	3 qt 6 oz	3 qt 16 oz	4 qt
Apples, diced	6 oz	12 oz	1 pt 4 oz	1 pt 8 oz	1 qt	1 qt 6 oz	1 qt 12 oz	1 qt 16 oz	1 qt 24 oz	2 qt
Bananas, sliced	6 oz	12 oz	1 pt 4 oz	1 pt 8 oz	1 qt	1 qt 6 oz	1 qt 12 oz	1 qt 16 oz	1 qt 24 oz	2 qt
Fruit, for garnish										

Nutrient Analysis per serving

Protein:	0.8 g
Carbohydrate:	13 g
Fat:	0.2 g
Sodium:	1 mg
Kilocalories:	53

Procedure

1. Mix all ingredients together and chill.

Note: Any colorful and contrasting fruit in season may be used for garnish (fresh strawberries, grapes, blueberries, melon balls, etc.). Sherbet is also often used with fruit cups.

FROSTED LIME MOLD

CATEGORY: Salad   PORTION: 2" × 2" square

INGREDIENTS	10	20	30	40	50	60	70	80	90	100
Lime Gelatin	4 oz	8 oz	12 oz	1 lb	1 lb 4 oz	1 lb 8 oz	1 lb 12 oz	2 lb	2 lb 4 oz	2 lb 8 oz
Water, boiling	8 oz	1 pt	1 pt 8 oz	1 qt 6 oz	1 qt 16 oz	1 qt 24 oz	2 qt	2 qt 8 oz	2 qt 24 oz	3 qt
Pineapple, crushed	1 pt	1 qt	1 qt 16 oz	2 qt	2 qt 16 oz	3 qt	3 qt 16 oz	4 qt	4 qt 16 oz	5 qt 8 oz
Vinegar	2 T	¼ C	⅓ C	½ C	¾ C	¾ C	⅔ C	1 C	1¼ C	1½ C
Salt	¼ t	½ t	¾ t	1 t	1½ t	1¾ t	2 t	2¼ t	2½ t	3 t
Carrots, shredded	2 oz	6 oz	8 oz	12 oz	1 pt	1 pt 2 oz	1 pt 6 oz	1 pt 8 oz	1 pt 12 oz	1 qt
Cabbage, shredded	2 oz	6 oz	8 oz	12 oz	1 pt	1 pt 2 oz	1 pt 6 oz	1 pt 8 oz	1 pt 12 oz	1 qt
Celery, thinly sliced	2 oz	6 oz	8 oz	12 oz	1 pt	1 pt 2 oz	1 pt 6 oz	1 pt 8 oz	1 pt 12 oz	1 qt
Salad Dressing	½ C	¾ C	1 C	1¼ C	1½ C	2 C	2¼ C	2½ C	2¾ C	3 C

Nutrient Analysis per serving

Protein:	2 g
Carbohydrate:	26 g
Fat:	9 g
Sodium:	188 mg
Kilocalories:	185

Procedure

1. Dissolve gelatin in boiling water.
2. Stir in undrained pineapple, vinegar, and salt.
3. Cool until mixture begins to thicken slightly.
4. Fold vegetables into gelatin.
5. Place ¾ of mixture in 2" steamtable pans.
6. Mix salad dressing into remaining gelatin mixture. Pour over the other gelatin pans. Spread evenly.
7. Chill until firm.
8. Cut into 2" squares.

Breads, Soups, and Salads   57

GARDEN COTTAGE CHEESE

CATEGORY: *Salad*   PORTION: ½ C, #8 dipper

INGREDIENTS	10	20	30	40	50	60	70	80	90	100
Radishes, chopped	¼ C	⅓ C	½ C	¾ C	1 C	1¼ C	1⅓ C	1½ C	1¾ C	2 C
Green Onions, chopped	2 T	¼ C	½ C	⅔ C	¾ C	¾ C	1 C	1¼ C	1⅓ C	1½ C
Celery, chopped	⅓ C	⅔ C	1 C	1½ C	2 C	2⅓ C	2⅔ C	3 C	3½ C	4 C
Green Peppers, chopped	¼ C	⅓ C	½ C	¾ C	1 C	1¼ C	1⅓ C	1½ C	1¾ C	2 C
Cucumbers, diced	2 oz	6 oz	8 oz	12 oz	1 lb	1 lb 2 oz	1 lb 6 oz	1 lb 10 oz	1 lb 12 oz	2 lb
Mayonnaise	4 oz	6 oz	8 oz	12 oz	1 pt	1 pt 4 oz	1 pt 6 oz	1 pt 10 oz	1 pt 12 oz	1 qt
Cottage Cheese	1 lb 4 oz	2 lb 8 oz	3 lb 12 oz	5 lb	6 lb 8 oz	7 lb 12 oz	9 lb	10 lb	11 lb 8 oz	13 lb
Seasoned Salt	½ t	1 t	1½ t	2 t	3 t	3½ t	4 t	5 t	5½ t	6 t

Nutrient Analysis per serving

Protein:	7 g
Carbohydrate:	3 g
Fat:	12 g
Sodium:	409 mg
Kilocalories:	142

Procedure

1. Combine all vegetables and toss lightly.
2. Add salad dressing to vegetables and mix lightly.
3. Stir in cottage cheese and mix lightly but well.
4. Refrigerate until served.
5. Prepare as close to serving as possible.

MARINATED CARROTS

INGREDIENTS	10	20	30	40	50	60	70	80	90	100
Pimientos	¼ C	½ C	¾ C	1¼ C	1½ C	1¾ C	2 C	2½ C	2¾ C	3 C
Onion Flakes	2 T	¼ C	⅓ C	½ C	⅔ C	¾ C	1 C	1¼ C	1⅓ C	1½ C
Tomato Soup	12 oz	1 pt 8 oz	1 qt	1 qt 16 oz	2 qt 8 oz	2 qt 24 oz	3 qt 8 oz	3 qt 24 oz	4 qt	4 qt 16 oz
Oil	¼ C	½ C	¾ C	1¼ C	1½ C	1¾ C	2 C	2¼ C	2¾ C	3 C
Sugar	½ C	1 C	1¼ C	2 C	2½ C	3 C	3½ C	3¾ C	4½ C	5 C
Vinegar	½ C	1 C	1¼ C	2 C	2½ C	3 C	3½ C	3¾ C	4½ C	5 C
Carrots, frozen sliced, cooked	2 lb 8 oz	4 lb 8 oz	7 lb 8 oz	10 lb	12 lb 8 oz	15 lb	17 lb 8 oz	18 lb	22 lb 8 oz	25 lb
Mustard, prepared	1½ t	1 T	1½ T	2 T	3 T	3½ T	4 T	4½ T	5 T	6 T
Worcestershire Sauce	1½ t	1 T	1½ T	2 T	3 T	3½ T	4 T	4½ T	5 T	6 T

Nutrient Analysis per serving

Protein:	1 g
Carbohydrate:	26 g
Fat:	7 g
Sodium:	77 mg
Kilocalories:	179

Procedure

1. Place layers of carrots, pimientos, and onions in pans.
2. Make marinade of remaining ingredients, beating until completely blended.
3. Pour over carrots and refrigerate overnight.

ONE CUP SALAD

INGREDIENTS	10	20	30	40	50	60	70	80	90	100
Fruit Cocktail, drained	1 C	2 C	3 C	4 C	5 C	6 C	7 C	8 C	9 C	10 C
Pineapple, crushed, drained	1 C	2 C	3 C	4 C	5 C	6 C	7 C	8 C	9 C	10 C
Marshmallows, miniature	1 C	2 C	3 C	4 C	5 C	6 C	7 C	8 C	9 C	10 C
Cottage Cheese or Yogurt	1 C	2 C	3 C	4 C	5 C	6 C	7 C	8 C	9 C	10 C
Coconut	1 C	2 C	3 C	4 C	5 C	6 C	7 C	8 C	9 C	10 C
Sour Cream	1 C	2 C	3 C	4 C	5 C	6 C	7 C	8 C	9 C	10 C

Nutrient Analysis per serving

Protein:	3 g
Carbohydrate:	12 g
Fat:	5 g
Sodium:	101 mg
Kilocalories:	115

Procedure

1. Mix all ingredients.
2. Chill well in refrigerator overnight.

PARMESAN PEA SALAD

CATEGORY: *Salad*   PORTION: *#8 scoop*

INGREDIENTS	10	20	30	40	50	60	70	80	90	100
Lettuce Heads, coarsely shredded	1	2	3	4	5	6	7	8	9	10
Frozen Peas, thawed	1 lb	2 lb	3 lb	4 lb	5 lb	6 lb	7 lb	8 lb	9 lb	10 lb
Stalk of Celery, diced	1	2	3	4	5	6	7	8	9	10
Medium Onion, diced	1	2	3	4	5	6	7	8	9	10
Parmesan Cheese	¼ C	½ C	¾ C	1 C	1¼ C	1½ C	1¾ C	2 C	2¼ C	2½ C
TOPPING:										
Mayonnaise	1⅓ C	1⅔ C	1 pt	1 pt 12 oz	1 pt 24 oz	1 qt	1 qt 12 oz	1 qt 24 oz	3 pt	3 pt 12 oz
Sugar	1 T	2 T	3 T	¼ C	⅓ C	⅓ C	½ C	½ C	⅔ C	⅔ C
Lemon Juice	1 T	2 T	3 T	¼ C	⅓ C	⅓ C	½ C	½ C	⅔ C	⅔ C

Nutrient Analysis per serving

Protein:	4 g
Carbohydrate:	11 g
Fat:	18 g
Sodium:	228 mg
Kilocalories:	226

Procedure

1. Arrange vegetables and cheese in layers with topping after each sequence.

PEA AND CHEESE SALAD

CATEGORY: Salad   PORTION: ½ C, #8 dipper

INGREDIENTS	10	20	30	40	50	60	70	80	90	100
Salad Dressing	4 oz	8 oz	12 oz	1 pt	1 pt 8 oz	1 pt 12 oz	1 qt	1 qt 4 oz	1 qt 8 oz	1 qt 16 oz
Onions, chopped	¼ C	⅓ C	½ C	¾ C	1 C	1¼ C	1⅓ C	1½ C	1¾ C	2 C
Celery, chopped	⅓ C	⅔ C	1 C	1½ C	2 C	2⅓ C	2⅔ C	3 C	3½ C	4 C
Pickle Relish	⅓ C	⅔ C	1 C	1½ C	2 C	2⅓ C	2⅔ C	3 C	3½ C	4 C
Pimientos	1 T	2 T	3 T	3½ T	4 T	5 T	6 T	6½ T	7 T	8 T
Eggs, hard-cooked	4	7	10	14	18	22	25	28	32	36
American Cheese, cubed	6 oz	12 oz	1 lb 2 oz	1 lb 8 oz	2 lb	2 lb 6 oz	2 lb 12 oz	3 lb 2 oz	3 lb 10 oz	4 lb
Peas, canned, drained	1 pt	1 qt	1 qt 16 oz	2 qt	3 qt	3 qt 16 oz	4 qt	4 qt 16 oz	5 qt	6 qt

Nutrient Analysis per serving

Protein:	8 g
Carbohydrate:	9 g
Fat:	15 g
Sodium:	428 mg
Kilocalories:	204

Procedure

1. Combine salad dressing, onions, celery, pickle relish, pimientos, and salt in a large mixing bowl. Stir to blend well.
2. Add cheese and mix well.
3. Add eggs and peas to salad dressing mixture. Mix lightly. Cover and refrigerate until served.

PINEAPPLE COTTAGE CHEESE

INGREDIENTS	10	20	30	40	50	60	70	80	90	100
Lettuce, washed, cleaned, trimmed (approx.)	1	2	3	4	5	6	7	8	9	10
Pineapple Slices	10	20	30	40	50	60	70	80	90	100
Cottage Cheese	10 oz	1 lb 4 oz	1 lb 14 oz	2 lb 8 oz	3 lb	3 lb 10 oz	4 lb 4 oz	4 lb 14 oz	5 lb 8 oz	6 lb
French Dressing	10 oz	1 pt 4 oz	1 qt	1 qt 8 oz	1 qt 16 oz	1 qt 24 oz	2 qt	2 qt 8 oz	2 qt 20 oz	3 qt
Maraschino Cherries (with stems)	10	20	30	40	50	60	70	80	90	100

Nutrient Analysis per serving

Protein:	4 g
Carbohydrate:	17 g
Fat:	19 g
Sodium:	508 mg
Kilocalories:	259

Procedure

1. Separate lettuce leaves to make lettuce cups. Place each on salad plate.
2. Place one slice pineapple in each cup.
3. Place small spoonful (1 oz) cottage cheese in center of each pineapple slice.
4. Dress with about 1 oz French dressing. Garnish with cherry.

SEVEN-LAYER SALAD

CATEGORY: Salad   PORTION: ½ C, #8 dipper

INGREDIENTS	10	20	30	40	50	60	70	80	90	100
Lettuce, chopped	1 lb 6 oz	2 lb 12 oz	4 lb	7 lb	8 lb 12 oz	10 lb 8 oz	11 lb	14 lb	15 lb 12 oz	17 lb 12 oz
Peas, frozen	4 oz	8 oz	12 oz	1 lb	1 lb 4 oz	1 lb 8 oz	1 lb 12 oz	2 lb	2 lb 4 oz	2 lb 8 oz
Bacon	4 oz	6 oz	8 oz	12 oz	1 lb	1 lb 4 oz	1 lb 6 oz	1 lb 8 oz	1 lb 12 oz	2 lb
Onion, finely chopped	1½ T	2 T	¼ C	⅓ C	½ C	½ C	⅔ C	¾ C	¾ C	1 C
Salad Dressing	3 oz	6 oz	8 oz	12 oz	1 pt	1 pt 2 oz	1 pt 6 oz	1 pt 8 oz	1 pt 12 oz	1 qt
Sugar	1 T	1 oz	1½ oz	2 oz	3 oz	3½ oz	4 oz	5 oz	5½ oz	6 oz
Parmesan Cheese	2 T	¼ C	⅓ C	½ C	¾ C	⅔ C	1 C	1¼ C	1⅓ C	1½ C

Nutrient Analysis per serving

Protein:	5 g
Carbohydrate:	4 g
Fat:	12 g
Sodium:	277 mg
Kilocalories:	153

Procedure

1. Place chopped lettuce in bottom of 1½" deep pan.
2. Sprinkle bacon over lettuce. Sprinkle peas over bacon and lettuce. Add a layer of chopped onion.
3. Mix sugar with salad dressing and pour over lettuce.
4. Cover with a layer of Parmesan cheese.
5. Place plastic wrap over salad and refrigerate overnight.

TOMATOES VINAIGRETTE

CATEGORY: Salad   PORTION: 2 to 3 slices

INGREDIENTS	10	20	30	40	50	60	70	80	90	100
Salt	½ t	1 t	1½ t	2 t	3 t	4 t	4½ t	5 t	5½ t	6 t
Sugar	⅛ t	¼ t	½ t	¾ t	1 t	1⅛ t	1¼ t	1½ t	1¾ t	2 t
Lemon Juice	2 oz	3 oz	4 oz	6 oz	8 oz	10 oz	12 oz	14 oz	15 oz	16 oz
Salad Oil	4 oz	8 oz	12 oz	1 pt	1 pt 8 oz	1 pt 12 oz	1 qt	1 qt 4 oz	1 qt 8 oz	1 qt 12 oz
Garlic Powder	⅛ t	¼ t	½ t	¾ t	1 t	1⅛ t	1¼ t	1½ t	1¾ t	2 t
Basil, dried	1 t	2 t	3 t	4 t	5 t	6 t	7 t	8 t	9 t	10 t
Parsley	½ T	1 T	1½ T	2 T	2½ T	3 T	3½ T	4 T	4½ T	5 T
Thyme, dried	¼ t	½ t	1 t	1½ t	2 t	2¼ t	2½ t	3 t	3¼ t	3½ t
Tomatoes, sliced	2 lb	4 lb	6 lb	8 lb	10 lb	12 lb	14 lb	16 lb	18 lb	20 lb

Nutrient Analysis per serving

Protein:	8 g
Carbohydrate:	4 g
Fat:	11 g
Sodium:	118 mg
Kilocalories:	115

Procedure

1. Mix all ingredients except tomatoes in a bowl.
2. Slice tomatoes.
3. Pour dressing over tomatoes.
4. Chill at least 2 hours.
5. Serve on lettuce.

CHAPTER 5

Entrées

BARBECUED SHORT RIBS

CATEGORY: *Entrée* PORTION: *8 oz*

INGREDIENTS	10	20	30	40	50	60	70	80	90	100
Beef Short Ribs	5 lb	10 lb	15 lb	20 lb	25 lb	30 lb	35 lb	40 lb	45 lb	50 lb
Barbecue Sauce	1 qt	1 qt	1 qt 16 oz	2 qt	2 qt 16 oz	3 qt	3 qt 16 oz	4 qt	4 qt 16 oz	5 qt

Nutrient Analysis per serving

Protein:	17 g
Carbohydrate:	6 g
Fat:	69 g
Sodium:	618 mg
Kilocalories:	938

Procedure

1. Place ribs in roasting pan and brown uncovered in oven at 350°F about 30 minutes. Pour off excess fat.
2. Pour barbecue sauce over ribs. Cover with aluminum foil. Bake at 350°F until meat is tender, about 1½ hours.
3. Uncover and bake an additional 20 to 30 minutes.

BEEF NOODLE CASSEROLE

CATEGORY: *Entrée*   PORTION: *6 oz*

INGREDIENTS	10	20	30	40	50	60	70	80	90	100
Beef, ground	2 lb 8 oz	5 lb	7 lb 8 oz	10 lb	12 lb 8 oz	15 lb	17 lb 8 oz	20 lb	22 lb 8 oz	25 lb
Margarine	4 oz	8 oz	1 lb	1 lb 4 oz	1 lb 8 oz	1 lb 12 oz	2 lb	2 lb 8 oz	2 lb 12 oz	3 lb
Onion, chopped	1	2	3	4	5	6	7	8	9	10
Green Pepper, chopped	1	2	3	4	5	6	7	8	9	10
Garlic, powdered	¼ t	½ t	¾ t	1 t	1¼ t	1½ t	1¾ t	2 t	2¼ t	2½ t
Sugar	1 T	1 oz	2 oz	3 oz	4 oz	5 oz	6 oz	7 oz	8 oz	9 oz
Worcestershire Sauce	1 oz	2 oz	3 oz	4 oz	5 oz	6 oz	7 oz	8 oz	9 oz	10 oz
Tomato Sauce, canned	1 pt 2 oz	1 qt 4 oz	1 qt 24 oz	2 qt 8 oz	2 qt 24 oz	3 qt 12 oz	4 qt	4 qt 16 oz	5 qt	5 qt 16 oz
Thin Noodles, cooked	8 oz	1 lb 4 oz	2 lb	2 lb 8 oz	3 lb 2 oz	3 lb 12 oz	4 lb 6 oz	5 lb 2 oz	5 lb 10 oz	6 lb 4 oz
Cream Cheese	8 oz	1 lb 4 oz	2 lb	2 lb 8 oz	2 lb 16 oz	2 lb 24 oz	3 lb 16 oz	4 lb 16 oz	4 lb 24 oz	5 lb
Sour Cream	1 pt 4 oz	1 qt 8 oz	2 qt	2 qt 16 oz	3 qt 4 oz	3 qt 24 oz	1 gal 12 oz	1 gal 1 qt	1 gal 2 qt	1 gal 3 qt
Cheddar Cheese	8 oz	1 lb 4 oz	2 lb	2 lb 8 oz	3 lb 2 oz	3 lb 12 oz	4 lb 6 oz	5 lb 2 oz	5 lb 8 oz	6 lb 4 oz

Nutrient Analysis per serving

Protein:	33 g
Carbohydrate:	16 g
Fat:	63 g
Sodium:	785 mg
Kilocalories:	763

Procedure

1. Sauté onion, green pepper, and garlic in margarine until soft.
2. Add beef and break up with a spoon. Drain off grease.
3. Add sugar, worcestershire, tomato sauce, salt, and pepper to taste.
4. Simmer covered for 1 hour.
5. Combine cream cheese and sour cream and beat at low speed until well blended.
6. In a greased rectangular baking pan layer half the noodles, half the sour cream mixture, and half the meat sauce. Repeat.
7. Sprinkle with cheese and bake at 350°F for 30 minutes.

BEEF POT PIE

CATEGORY: *Entrée*   PORTION: *8 oz*

INGREDIENTS	10	20	30	40	50	60	70	80	90	100
Beef Chuck, cubed	1 lb 8 oz	3 lb	4 lb 8 oz	6 lb	7 lb 8 oz	9 lb	10 lb 8 oz	12 lb	13 lb 8 oz	15 lb
Flour	¼ C	½ C	¾ C	1 C	1¼ C	1½ C	1¾ C	2 C	2¼ C	2½ C
Corn Oil	2 oz	4 oz	6 oz	8 oz	10 oz	12 oz	14 oz	1 lb	1 lb 2 oz	1 lb 4 oz
Cloves of Garlic, minced	1	1	1	2 cloves	2 cloves	2 cloves	3 cloves	3 cloves	3 cloves	4 cloves
Medium Onions, chopped	1	2	3	4	5	6	7	8	9	10
Salt	1 t	2 t	3 t	4 t	5 t	6 t	7 t	8 t	9 t	10 t
Pepper	¼ t	½ t	¾ t	1 t	1¼ t	1½ t	1¾ t	2 t	2¼ t	2½ t
Parsley Sprigs, chopped	2	4	6	8	10	12	14	16	18	20
Tomatoes, chopped	1	2	3	4	5	6	7	8	9	10
Stock to cover	1 qt 6 oz	2 qt 12 oz	1 gal	1 gal 1 qt	1 gal 2 qt	1 gal 3 qt	2 gal 1 qt	2 gal 2 qt	2 gal 3 qt	3 gal
Carrots, fresh, sliced	10 oz	1 lb 4 oz	1 lb 14 oz	2 lb 8 oz	3 lb	3 lb 10 oz	4 lb 4 oz	4 lb 14 oz	5 lb 8 oz	6 lb
Potatoes, fresh, cubed	1 lb	2 lb	3 lb	4 lb	5 lb	6 lb	7 lb	8 lb	9 lb	10 lb

Nutrient Analysis per serving

Protein:	20.3 g
Carbohydrate:	11.3 g
Fat:	11.0 g
Sodium:	557 mg
Kilocalories:	225

Procedure

1. Dredge meat in flour; brown in hot shortening.
2. Add garlic, onions, salt, pepper, parsley, tomatoes, and stock. Cover and simmer for 2½ hours or until meat is tender.
3. Add carrots and potatoes. Cook 30 minutes or until vegetables are tender.
4. Place in baking pan and top with pastry crust *or* biscuits.
5. Bake in 350°F oven until topping is browned.

BEEF STEAK PATTIES

INGREDIENTS	10	20	30	40	50	60	70	80	90	100
Beef, ground	3 lb 12 oz	7 lb 8 oz	11 lb 6 oz	16 lb 4 oz	19 lb	22 lb 12 oz	26 lb 8 oz	30 lb 6 oz	35 lb 4 oz	38 lb
Salad oil to lightly coat										

Nutrient Analysis per serving

Protein:	33 g
Carbohydrate:	0
Fat:	28 g
Sodium:	106 mg
Kilocalories:	398

Procedure

1. Scale ground meat into 6 oz portions and form into oval patties.
2. Dip patties in oil and place on preheated broiler rack.
3. When lightly browned, turn carefully, using a spatula or meat turner. Broiler marks should show on meat. Brown second side and remove to bake sheet or other pan when still rare. Finish in oven or return to broiler at service time.

Note: Patties may be served with appropriate sauce, onion rings, or brushed with butter and sprinkled with fresh chopped parsley.

BEEFY MACARONI CASSEROLE

INGREDIENTS	10	20	30	40	50	60	70	80	90	100
Macaroni, elbow, uncooked	8 oz	1 lb 4 oz	2 lb	2 lb 8 oz	3 lb 4 oz	4 lb	4 lb 8 oz	5 lb	6 lb	6 lb 8 oz
Beef, ground, lean	2 lb	3 lb 8 oz	5 lb 8 oz	7 lb 8 oz	9 lb 8 oz	11 lb	13 lb	15 lb	16 lb 8 oz	19 lb
Onions, finely chopped	8 oz	1 lb 4 oz	2 lb	2 lb 8 oz	3 lb 4 oz	4 lb	4 lb 8 oz	5 lb	6 lb	6 lb 8 oz
Tomato soup, condensed	1 qt	2 qt	3 qt	4 qt	5 qt	6 qt	7 qt	8 qt	9 qt	10 qt
Vinegar, cider	1½ T	2½ T	¼ C	⅓ C	6½ T	½ C	9 T	⅔ C	¾ C	1 C
Worcestershire Sauce	2 t	4 t	2 T	2½ T	3 T	3½ T	4 T	4½ T	5 T	5½ T
Salt	1 t	2 t	1 T	4 t	5 t	2 T	7 t	8 t	3 T	10 t
Pepper	⅛ t	¼ t	½ t	¾ t	1 t	1⅛ t	1¼ t	1½ t	1¾ t	2 t
Parmesan Cheese	¼ C	½ C	¾ C	¾ C	1 C	1½ C	1¾ C	2 C	2¼ C	2½ C

Nutrient Analysis per serving

Protein:	21 g
Carbohydrate:	20 g
Fat:	14 g
Sodium:	894 mg
Kilocalories:	297

Procedure

1. Cook macaroni according to package directions. Drain.
2. Brown beef slowly in heavy skillet. Add onion; cook until tender.
3. Blend in soup, vinegar, seasonings, and cooked macaroni.
4. Pour into baking pans. Sprinkle with cheese.
5. Bake in 350°F oven 45 minutes or until lightly browned.

CHEESEBURGER PIE

INGREDIENTS	10	20	30	40	50	60	70	80	90	100
Beef, ground	2 lb	4 lb	6 lb	8 lb	10 lb	12 lb	14 lb	16 lb	18 lb	20 lb
Onions, chopped	4 oz	8 oz	1 lb	1 lb 4 oz	1 lb 8 oz	2 lb	2 lb 4 oz	2 lb 8 oz	3 lb	3 lb 4 oz
Salt	½ t	1 t	1½ t	2 t	2½ t	3 t	3½ t	4 t	4½ t	5 t
Pepper	⅛ t	¼ t	½ t	¾ t	1 t	1⅛ t	1¼ t	1½ t	1¾ t	2 t
Milk	12 oz	1 pt 8 oz	1 qt 6 oz	1 qt 16 oz	2 qt	2 qt 12 oz	2 qt 24 oz	3 qt 6 oz	3 qt 16 oz	1 gal
Biscuit Mix	4 oz	6 oz	8 oz	12 oz	1 lb	1 lb 2 oz	1 lb 6 oz	1 lb 8 oz	1 lb 12 oz	2 lb
Eggs	3	6	9	12	15	18	21	24	27	30
Tomatoes, sliced, fresh	8 oz	1 lb	1 lb 8 oz	2 lb	3 lb	3 lb 8 oz	4 lb	4 lb 8 oz	5 lb	6 lb
American Cheese, grated	4 oz	8 oz	12 oz	1 lb	1 lb 4 oz	1 lb 8 oz	1 lb 12 oz	2 lb	2 lb 4 oz	2 lb 8 oz

Nutrient Analysis per serving

Protein:	22 g
Carbohydrate:	9 g
Fat:	25 g
Sodium:	434 mg
Kilocalories:	361

Procedure

1. Brown beef and onions. Drain well. Stir in salt and pepper.
2. Spread in greased baking pan.
3. Beat milk, biscuit mix, and eggs until smooth in food processor. Pour into pan.
4. Bake at 400°F for 25 minutes.
5. Top with tomatoes; sprinkle with cheese.
6. Baked until knife inserted in center comes out clean.

CRISP BAKED VEAL

CATEGORY: Entrée   PORTION: 3 oz

INGREDIENTS	10	20	30	40	50	60	70	80	90	100
Veal Patty, 4 oz raw	10	20	30	40	50	60	70	80	90	100
Vegetable Oil	4 oz	8 oz	12 oz	1 pt	24 oz	1 pt 12 oz	1 qt	1 qt 4 oz	1 qt 8 oz	1 qt 16 oz
Corn Flake Crumbs	1 pt	1 qt	1 qt 16 oz	2 qt	2 qt 16 oz	3 qt	3 qt 8 oz	3 qt 16 oz	4 qt 16 oz	1 gal 32 oz
Salt	1½ t	1 T	1½ T	2 T	2½ T	3 T	3½ T	4 T	4½ T	5 T
Paprika	½ t	¾ t	1¼ t	1½ t	2 t	2½ t	2¾ t	3¼ t	3½ t	4 t
White Pepper	½ t	1 t	1½ t	2 t	2½ t	3 t	3½ t	4 t	4½ t	5 t

Nutrient Analysis per serving

Protein:	22 g
Carbohydrate:	5 g
Fat:	21 g
Sodium:	488 mg
Kilocalories:	310

Procedure

1. Dip each veal patty in oil and drain well in a colander.
2. Mix corn flake crumbs, salt, paprika, and pepper together; place on baking sheet.
3. Dredge veal in seasoned crumbs; put on a well-greased pan and be careful not to crowd.
4. Bake at 350°F for 25 to 30 minutes or until done.

74   *Recipes*

CUBE STEAK ITALIAN

INGREDIENTS	10	20	30	40	50	60	70	80	90	100
Eggs	2	4	6	7	8	10	12	14	15	16
Pepper, white	dash	dash	⅛ t	⅛ t	¼ t	¼ t	⅓ t	⅓ t	½ t	½ t
Water	1 oz	2 oz	3 oz	4 oz	5 oz	6 oz	8 oz	8 oz	10 oz	12 oz
Beef Cube Steak	2 lb	4 lb	6 lb	8 lb	11 lb	13 lb	15 lb	17 lb	19 lb	22 lb
Saltine Crackers, finely crushed	4 oz	6 oz	8 oz	12 oz	1 lb	1 lb 4 oz	1 lb 6 oz	1 lb 8 oz	1 lb 12 oz	2 lb
Parmesan Cheese	2 oz	3 oz	4 oz	6 oz	8 oz	10 oz	12 oz	14 oz	1 lb	1 lb 2 oz
Vegetable Oil	2 oz	4 oz	6 oz	8 oz	10 oz	12 oz	1 pt	1 pt 2 oz	1 pt 4 oz	1 pt 6 oz
Pizza Sauce	8 oz	1 pt	1 pt 8 oz	1 qt	1 qt 8 oz	1 qt 16 oz	1 qt 24 oz	2 qt	2 qt 8 oz	2 qt 16 oz
Parmesan Cheese	2 oz	3 oz	4 oz	6 oz	8 oz	10 oz	12 oz	14 oz	1 lb	1 lb 2 oz

Nutrient Analysis per serving

Protein:	27 g
Carbohydrate:	10 g
Fat:	26 g
Sodium:	389 mg
Kilocalories:	403

Procedure

1. Beat together eggs, pepper, and water.
2. Dip beef in the egg mixture.
3. Combine crumbs and cheese. Roll beef in mixture and brown in hot oil in skillet.
4. Place browned steaks in baking pan and pour pizza sauce over to cover.
5. Sprinkle with Parmesan cheese. Cover and bake in 350°F oven for 1 hour.

DEVILED BEEF PATTIES

CATEGORY: *Entrée*   PORTION: 1

INGREDIENTS	10	20	30	40	50	60	70	80	90	100
Beef, ground	2 lb 8 oz	5 lb	7 lb 8 oz	10 lb	12 lb 8 oz	15 lb	17 lb 8 oz	20 lb	22 lb 8 oz	25 lb
Eggs	2	4	6	8	10	12	14	16	18	20
Ketchup	½ C	1 C	1½ C	2 C	2½ C	3 C	3½ C	4 C	4½ C	5 C
Mustard, prepared	2 t	4 t	2 T	2½ T	3 T	3½ T	4 T	4½ T	5 T	6 T
Onion, instant, minced	2 t	4 t	2 T	2½ T	3 T	3½ T	4 T	4½ T	5 T	6 T
Worcestershire Sauce	2 t	4 t	2 T	2½ T	3 T	3½ T	4 T	4½ T	5 T	6 T
Salt	1 t	2 t	3 t	4 t	5 t	6 t	7 t	8 t	9 t	10 t
Pepper	dash	¼ t	½ t	¾ t	1 t	1⅛ t	1¼ t	1½ t	1¾ t	2 t

Nutrient Analysis per serving

Protein: 23 g
Carbohydrate: 3 g
Fat: 17 g
Sodium: 343 mg
Kilocalories: 273

Procedure

1. Combine all ingredients in mixing bowl. Mix well.
2. Shape into patties.
3. Broil 3 inches from heat for 5 minutes; turn and broil 4 minutes longer or until done.
4. Serve on plain, toasted ½ hamburger bun.

GOURMET SWISS STEAK

CATEGORY: *Entrée*   PORTION: *3 oz steak, 1 oz sauce*

INGREDIENTS	10	20	30	40	50	60	70	80	90	100
Salisbury Steak, 3 oz	10	20	30	40	50	60	70	80	90	100
Tomato, diced	8 oz	1 lb	1 lb 4 oz	1 lb 12 oz	2 lb 4 oz	2 lb 8 oz	2 lb 12 oz	3 lb 4 oz	3 lb 12 oz	4 lb 8 oz
Green Pepper, dehydrated	1 T	2 T	3 T	4 T	5 T	6 T	7 T	8 T	9 T	10 T
Onions, dehydrated	1 T	2 T	3 T	4 T	5 T	6 T	7 T	8 T	9 T	10 T
Celery, diced	1 oz	2 oz	3 oz	4 oz	5 oz	6 oz	7 oz	8 oz	9 oz	10 oz
Worcestershire Sauce	1 t	2 t	2½ t	3 t	4 t	5 t	6 t	7 t	8 t	9 t
Gravy	12 oz	1 pt 8 oz	1 qt 6 oz	1 qt 16 oz	2 qt	2 qt 12 oz	3 qt	3 qt 6 oz	3 qt 12 oz	1 gal

Nutrient Analysis per serving

Protein:	27 g
Carbohydrate:	4 g
Fat:	11 g
Sodium:	411 mg
Kilocalories:	242

Procedure

1. Thaw meat, dredge in flour.
2. Layer in oiled sheet pans.
3. Bake at 350°F for 5 minutes or until brown.
4. Transfer meat to 6" deep steamtable pans.
5. Combine ingredients for sauce and pour over cooked meat.
6. Cover tightly with foil, bake 1½ to 2 hours at 325°F.
7. Add prepared gravy to mixture before serving.

IRISH STEW

INGREDIENTS	10	20	30	40	50	60	70	80	90	100
Stew Meat	2 lb 8 oz	5 lb	7 lb 8 oz	10 lb	12 lb 8 oz	15 lb	17 lb 8 oz	20 lb	22 lb 8 oz	25 lb
Irish Potatoes, whole	2 lb 8 oz	5 lb	7 lb 8 oz	10 lb	12 lb 8 oz	15 lb	17 lb 8 oz	20 lb	22 lb 8 oz	25 lb
Carrots, canned, sliced	1 lb 4 oz	2 lb 8 oz	3 lb 12 oz	5 lb	6 lb 4 oz	7 lb 8 oz	8 lb 12 oz	10 lb	11 lb 4 oz	12 lb 8 oz
Green Beans, canned	1 lb 4 oz	2 lb 8 oz	3 lb 12 oz	5 lb	6 lb 4 oz	7 lb 8 oz	8 lb 12 oz	10 lb	11 lb 4 oz	12 lb 8 oz
French Onion Soup, canned	1 pt	1 qt	1 qt 16 oz	2 qt	2 qt 16 oz	3 qt	3 qt 16 oz	4 qt	4 qt 16 oz	5 qt
Flour, all-purpose	½ C	1 C	2 C	2½ C	3 C	3½ C	4 C	5 C	5½ C	6 C
Water	2½ C	5 C	7½ C	10 C	12½ C	15 C	17½ C	20 C	22½ C	25 C

Nutrient Analysis per serving

Protein:	40 g
Carbohydrate:	33 g
Fat:	8 g
Sodium:	736 mg
Kilocalories:	368

Procedure

1. Brown stew meat in baking pans for 45 minutes, stirring occasionally.
2. Add potatoes, carrots, green beans, and French Onion soup to browned meat.
3. In a separate mixing bowl, mix flour with water. (If necessary, whip to remove lumps.)
4. Add flour and water mixture to stew and mix thoroughly.
5. Bake at 350°F for 1 hour.

MEATLOAF

CATEGORY: Entrée   PORTION: 3 oz

INGREDIENTS	10	20	30	40	50	60	70	80	90	100
Corn Flakes	2 oz	4 oz	8 oz	10 oz	12 oz	14 oz	1 lb	1 lb 2 oz	1 lb 4 oz	1 lb 8 oz
Eggs	2	4	6	8	10	12	14	16	18	20
Milk	6 oz	12 oz	1 pt 4 oz	1 pt 8 oz	1 qt	1 qt 6 oz	1 qt 12 oz	1 qt 16 oz	1 qt 24 oz	2 qt
Onion, chopped	1½ T	2½ T	¼ C	⅓ C	½ C	⅔ C	⅔ C	¾ C	¾ C	1 C
Worcestershire Sauce	1½ T	2½ T	¼ C	⅓ C	½ C	⅔ C	⅔ C	¾ C	¾ C	1 C
Mustard, dry	1¼ t	2½ t	4 t	5 t	2 T	2½ T	3 T	3½ T	3¾ T	4 T
Pepper	⅛ t	¼ t	½ t	¾ t	1 t	1⅛ t	1¼ t	1½ t	1¾ t	2 t
Salt	1 T	1½ T	2 T	3 T	4 T	5 T	6 T	7 T	8 T	9 T
Beef, ground	2 lb	4 lb	6 lb	8 lb	10 lb	12 lb	14 lb	16 lb	18 lb	20 lb

Nutrient Analysis per serving

Protein:	18 g
Carbohydrate:	6 g
Fat:	21 g
Sodium:	834 mg
Kilocalories:	298

Procedure

1. Place corn flakes, eggs, milk, onions, Worcestershire, mustard, pepper, and salt in large mixer bowl.
2. Mix on medium speed until combined.
3. Add ground beef to mixture.
4. Spread evenly in ungreased pans.
5. Bake in 350°F oven for 1½ hours.

MOCK FILET MIGNON

CATEGORY: *Entrée*   PORTION: *3 oz patty*

INGREDIENTS	10	20	30	40	50	60	70	80	90	100
Beef, ground	1 lb 12 oz	3 lb 8 oz	5 lb 6 oz	7 lb 2 oz	9 lb	10 lb 12 oz	12 lb 8 oz	14 lb 6 oz	16 lb 2 oz	18 lb
Rice, cooked	12 oz	24 oz	1 qt 4 oz	1 qt 16 oz	1 qt 24 oz	2 qt 4 oz	2 qt 8 oz	3 qt	3 qt 8 oz	3 qt 12 oz
Eggs	3	5	7	10	12	14	17	19	22	24
Onions, minced	6 oz	8 oz	1 lb 2 oz	1 lb 8 oz	2 lb	2 lb 6 oz	2 lb 12 oz	3 lb	3 lb 8 oz	4 lb
Salt	1 t	2 t	1 T	1½ T	2 T	2½ T	3 T	3½ T	4 T	4½ T
Pepper	¼ t	½ t	¾ t	1 t	1½ t	1¾ t	2 t	2¼ t	2½ t	3 t
Bacon, sliced	8 oz	1 lb 2 oz	1 lb 8 oz	2 lb 6 oz	3 lb	3 lb 8 oz	4 lb 2 oz	4 lb 12 oz	5 lb 6 oz	6 lb

Nutrient Analysis per serving

Protein:	20 g
Carbohydrate:	8 g
Fat:	40 g
Sodium:	554 mg
Kilocalories:	484

Procedure

1. Combine ingredients, except bacon. Mix well.
2. Form into steaks ¾" thick.
3. Wrap each with a slice of bacon. Secure with a toothpick.
4. Place on ungreased baking sheet.
5. Bake at 325°F for 2 to 2½ hours.

MUSHROOM STEAK

CATEGORY: *Entrée*   PORTION: *3 oz steak*

INGREDIENTS	10	20	30	40	50	60	70	80	90	100
Beef Patty, 3 oz	10	20	30	40	50	60	70	80	90	100
Mushroom Soup, canned	8 oz	1 pt 4 oz	1 qt	1 qt 8 oz	1 qt 16 oz	2 qt	2 qt 6 oz	2 qt 16 oz	2 qt 24 oz	3 qt
Milk	4 oz	8 oz	12 oz	1 pt	1 pt 8 oz	1 pt 12 oz	1 qt	1 qt 2 oz	1 qt 8 oz	1 qt 16 oz

Nutrient Analysis per serving

Protein:	17 g
Carbohydrate:	2 g
Fat:	15 g
Sodium:	289 mg
Kilocalories:	221

Procedure

1. Brown patties and place in baking pan.
2. Mix soup and milk together. Pour over meat.
3. Cover with foil and bake at 350°F for 1 hour.

OLD-FASHIONED POT ROAST

CATEGORY: *Entrée*   PORTION: *3 oz meat, ¾ C vegetable*

INGREDIENTS	10	20	30	40	50	60	70	80	90	100
Beef Round Roast, boneless	4 lb	8 lb	12 lb	16 lb	20 lb	24 lb	28 lb	32 lb	36 lb	40 lb
Shortening	2 oz	3 oz	4 oz	6 oz	8 oz	10 oz	11 oz	13 oz	14 oz	1 lb
Flour	2 oz	4 oz	8 oz	10 oz	12 oz	14 oz	1 lb	1 lb 2 oz	1 lb 4 oz	1 lb 8 oz
Water	12 oz	1 pt 8 oz	1 qt 4 oz	1 qt 20 oz	2 qt	2 qt 12 oz	2 qt 24 oz	3 qt 4 oz	3 qt 20 oz	4 qt
Carrots	2 lb	5 lb	7 lb	10 lb	12 lb	14 lb	17 lb	19 lb	22 lb	24 lb
Potatoes	2 lb	5 lb	7 lb	10 lb	12 lb	14 lb	17 lb	19 lb	22 lb	24 lb
Celery	6 oz	12 oz	1 lb	1 lb 8 oz	1 lb 14 oz	2 lb 4 oz	2 lb 10 oz	2 lb 14 oz	3 lb 6 oz	3 lb 12 oz
Salt	1 t	2 t	1 T	1¼ T	1½ T	2 T	2¼ T	2½ T	3 T	3½ T

Nutrient Analysis per serving

Protein:	44 g
Carbohydrate:	32 g
Fat:	13 g
Sodium:	234 mg
Kilocalories:	439

Procedure

1. Melt shortening in heavy kettle.
2. Flour meat and brown on all sides.
3. Season with salt.
4. Add water and simmer 2½ hours.
5. Partially cook vegetables for 10 minutes.
6. Add vegetables to stock and simmer for 1 additional hour; add water if needed.

OPEN-FACED PATTY MELT

INGREDIENTS	10	20	30	40	50	60	70	80	90	100
Beef, ground	1 lb 10 oz	3 lb 6 oz	4 lb	7 lb	8 lb 6 oz	10 lb	11 lb 12 oz	13 lb	15 lb 6 oz	16 lb 12 oz
American Cheese, ½ oz slices	10	20	30	40	50	60	70	80	90	100
Rye Bread	10	20	30	40	50	60	70	80	90	100
Onions, grilled										

Nutrient Analysis per serving

Protein:	18 g
Carbohydrate:	13 g
Fat:	20 g
Sodium:	389 mg
Kilocalories:	310

Procedure

1. Form raw ground beef into patties with a #12 scoop.
2. Bake patties in oven until almost done.
3. Place patties on bread on greased bun pan.
4. Melt cheese on patties the last 5 minutes of baking.
5. Serve open-faced on one slice of rye bread.
6. Top with grilled onions.

PEPPER STEAK

CATEGORY: Entrée   PORTION: 3 oz steak

INGREDIENTS	10	20	30	40	50	60	70	80	90	100
Beef Patty, 3 oz	10	20	30	40	50	60	70	80	90	100
Onions, sliced and separated	1	2	3	4	5	6	7	8	9	10
Green Pepper, sliced in rings, 10 oz	1	2	3	4	5	6	7	8	9	10
Tomato Soup	1 pt 4 oz	1 qt 10 oz	2 qt	2 qt 24 oz	3 qt 8 oz	4 qt	5 qt	5 qt 8 oz	6 qt	6 qt 4 oz
Water	1 pt 8 oz	1 qt 8 oz	2 qt	2 qt 16 oz	3 qt 8 oz	4 qt	5 qt	5 qt 8 oz	6 qt	6 qt 4 oz
Garlic Powder	½ t	¾ t	1 t	1⅛ t	1¼ t	1½ t	1¾ t	2 t	2¼ t	2½ t
Lemon Juice	2 T	3 T	¼ C	⅓ C	½ C	⅔ C	¾ C	1 C	1¼ C	1½ C

Nutrient Analysis per serving

Protein:	17 g
Carbohydrate:	9 g
Fat:	13 g
Sodium:	492 mg
Kilocalories:	230

Procedure

1. Brown beef patties in small amount of fat on top of stove or in the oven.
2. Drain and put patties in steamtable pan.
3. Place sliced onions and pepper on top of meat.
4. Mix soup, water, lemon juice, and garlic powder. Pour over meat patties and vegetables.
5. Cover with foil.

PIZZABURGER

CATEGORY: *Entrée*   PORTION: *2 oz*

INGREDIENTS	10	20	30	40	50	60	70	80	90	100
Cheese, grated	4 oz	8 oz	1 lb	1 lb 4 oz	1 lb 8 oz	2 lb	2 lb 4 oz	2 lb 8 oz	3 lb	3 lb 2 oz
Beef, ground	1 lb 2 oz	2 lb 6 oz	3 lb 8 oz	5 lb	6 lb	7 lb 2 oz	8 lb 6 oz	10 lb	11 lb	12 lb 14 oz
Pizza Sauce	1 pt 2 oz	1 qt 6 oz	1 qt 24 oz	2 qt 12 oz	3 qt	3 qt 16 oz	1 gal 6 oz	1 gal 24 oz	1 gal 1 qt	1 gal 2 qt
Hamburger Rolls	10	20	30	40	50	60	70	80	90	100

Nutrient Analysis per serving

Protein:	15 g
Carbohydrate:	31 g
Fat:	18 g
Sodium:	670 mg
Kilocalories:	356

Procedure

1. Brown and drain beef. Mix beef with pizza sauce. Refrigerate overnight in stainless steel pan to blend flavor of the spices.
2. Arrange opened rolls 4 × 6 on greased sheet pan.
3. Portion meat sauce with #16 scoop (¼ C). Divide each scoop of meat between top and bottom of a roll. Top with ¼ oz cheese on each half. Bake at 375°F for 9 to 10 minutes.

SALISBURY STEAK

CATEGORY: Entrée   PORTION: 2 to 3 oz

INGREDIENTS	10	20	30	40	50	60	70	80	90	100
Beef, ground	2 lb 4 oz	4 lb 8 oz	6 lb 12 oz	9 lb	11 lb 4 oz	13 lb 8 oz	15 lb 12 oz	18 lb	20 lb 4 oz	22 lb 8 oz
Salt	½ T	1 T	1½ T	2 T	2½ T	3 T	3½ T	4 T	4½ T	5 T
Pepper	½ t	1 t	1½ t	2 t	2½ t	1 T	1 T ½ t	1 T 1 t	2 T	2 T 1 t
Bread Crumbs	9 oz	1 lb 2 oz	1 lb 11 oz	2 lb 4 oz	2 lb 13 oz	3 lb 6 oz	3 lb 15 oz	4 lb 8 oz	5 lb	5 lb 9 oz
Onions, finely chopped	3 oz	6 oz	9 oz	12 oz	15 oz	1 lb 2 oz	1 lb 5 oz	1 lb 8 oz	1 lb 11 oz	1 lb 14 oz
Eggs	1	2	3	4	5	6	7	8	9	10
Water	¾ C	1½ C	2¼ C	3 C	3¾ C	4½ C	5¼ C	6 C	7 C	7¾ C

Nutrient Analysis per serving

Protein:	23 g
Carbohydrate:	13 g
Fat:	17 g
Sodium:	360 mg
Kilocalories:	311

Procedure

1. Combine ingredients in mixer bowl. Mix on low speed for 3 minutes.
2. Shape into oblong loaves—3 to a pound of raw mixture. Place on ungreased sheet pans.
3. Bake in 350°F oven 1 hour.
4. Serve with brown gravy.

SALISBURY STEAK ITALIANO

CATEGORY: *Entrée*   PORTION: *2 oz meat, ¼ C vegetable*

INGREDIENTS	10	20	30	40	50	60	70	80	90	100
Beef, ground	2 lb	4 lb	6 lb	8 lb	10 lb	12 lb	14 lb	16 lb	18 lb	20 lb
Bread Crumbs	⅓ C	¾ C	1¼ C	1½ C	2 C	2⅓ C	2¾ C	3¼ C	3½ C	4 C
Eggs	1	2	4	5	6	7	8	10	11	12
Tabasco	1¼ t	2½ t	1 T	1½ T	2 T	2½ T	3 T	3½ T	4 T	4 T
Water	½ C	1 C	1¼ C	2 C	3 C	3½ C	4 C	4¼ C	5 C	6 C
Salt	1¼ t	2½ t	1 T	1½ T	2 T	2½ T	3 T	3½ T	4 T	4 T
Parmesan Cheese, grated	2 oz	3 oz	4 oz	6 oz	8 oz	10 oz	11 oz	12 oz	14 oz	1 lb
Onions, chopped	¼ C	½ C	¾ C	1 C	1½ C	1¾ C	2 C	2¼ C	2½ C	3 C
Cooking Oil	¼ C	⅓ C	½ C	⅔ C	1 C	1¼ C	1⅓ C	1½ C	1⅔ C	2 C
Tomato Sauce	1 qt 16 oz	3 qt 6 oz	5 qt	6 qt	2 gal	2¼ gal	2½ gal	3 gal	3½ gal	4 gal
Oregano, crushed	1¼ t	2½ t	3 t	5 t	6 t	7 t	8 t	9½ t	10 t	12 t
Sugar	1¼ t	2½ t	3 t	5 t	6 t	7 t	8 t	9½ t	10 t	12 t

Nutrient Analysis per serving

Protein:	22 g
Carbohydrate:	15 g
Fat:	19 g
Sodium:	1230 mg
Kilocalories:	323

Procedure

1. Combine first six ingredients. Shape into oval patties.
2. Grill, broil, or bake in usual manner.
3. Combine the remaining ingredients to make the sauce. The ingredients should simmer for approximately 1 hour.

SAVORY STEAK

CATEGORY: Entrée   PORTION: 1

INGREDIENTS	10	20	30	40	50	60	70	80	90	100
Round or cube steaks, 3 oz	10	20	30	40	50	60	70	80	90	100
Flour, bread, seasoned	4 oz	6 oz	8 oz	12 oz	1 lb	1 lb 4 oz	1 lb 6 oz	1 lb 8 oz	1 lb 12 oz	2 lb
Salad Oil	6 oz	12 oz	1 lb 2 oz	1 lb 8 oz	1 qt	1 qt 6 oz	1 qt 12 oz	1 qt 16 oz	1 qt 24 oz	2 qt
Beef Stock	1 qt	2 qt	3 qt	1 gal	1 gal 1 qt	1 gal 2 qt	1 gal 3 qt	2 gal	2 gal 1 qt	2 gal 2 qt
Tomato Purée	2 oz	4 oz	6 oz	8 oz	10 oz	12 oz	14 oz	1 lb	1 lb 2 oz	1 lb 4 oz
Soy Sauce	1 oz	2 oz	3 oz	4 oz	5 oz	6 oz	7 oz	8 oz	9 oz	10 oz
Pepper, black	¼ t	½ t	¾ t	1 t	1¼ t	1½ t	1¾ t	2 t	2¼ t	2½ t
Whole Cloves	1	2	3	4	5	6	7	8	9	10
Bay Leaves	1	1	1	2	2	2	3	3	3	4
Salad Oil	2 oz	6 oz	8 oz	12 oz	1 pt	1 pt 2 oz	1 pt 6 oz	1 pt 8 oz	1 pt 12 oz	2 pt
Onions, diced	4 oz	6 oz	8 oz	12 oz	1 lb	1 lb 4 oz	1 lb 6 oz	1 lb 8 oz	1 lb 12 oz	2 lb
Celery, diced	2 oz	4 oz	6 oz	8 oz	10 oz	12 oz	14	1 lb	1 lb 2 oz	1 lb 4 oz
Flour	2 oz	4 oz	6 oz	8 oz	10 oz	12 oz	14 oz	1 lb	1 lb 2 oz	1 lb 4 oz
Salt	½ t	1 t	1½ t	2 t	2½ t	3 t	3½ t	4 t	4½ t	5 t

Nutrient Analysis per serving

Protein:	28 g
Carbohydrate:	15 g
Fat:	32 g
Sodium:	619 mg
Kilocalories:	467

Procedure

1. Dredge steaks in seasoned flour. Heat oil in skillet. Add steaks and brown. Place in baking pan.
2. Combine beef stock, tomato purée, soy sauce, black pepper, cloves, and bay leaves. Simmer for 20 minutes to make hot stock.
3. Sauté onions and celery in salad oil until tender. Add flour to make a roux. Stir and cook for 10 minutes, browning lightly.
4. Strain stock and add to roux, stirring until thickened and smooth. Pour sauce over steaks. Bake in 350°F oven 2 hours or until tender.

SPAGHETTI CASSEROLE

INGREDIENTS	10	20	30	40	50	60	70	80	90	100
Spaghetti, ready-cut	8 oz	1 lb	1 lb 4 oz	1 lb 12 oz	2 lb 4 oz	2 lb 8 oz	3 lb	4 lb	4 lb 4 oz	5 lb
Beef, ground	1 lb 4 oz	2 lb 8 oz	3 lb 12 oz	5 lb	6 lb 4 oz	7 lb 8 oz	8 lb 12 oz	10 lb	11 lb 4 oz	12 lb 8 oz
Celery, sliced	6 oz	12 oz	1 pt 2 oz	1 pt 8 oz	1 pt 12 oz	1 qt	1 qt 8 oz	1 qt 16 oz	1 qt 24 oz	2 qt
Onion, chopped	6 oz	12 oz	1 pt 2 oz	1 pt 8 oz	1 pt 12 oz	1 qt	1 qt 1 C	1 qt 2 C	1 qt 3 C	2 qt
Tomato Paste	6 oz	12 oz	1 pt 2 oz	1 pt 8 oz	1 pt 12 oz	1 qt	1 qt 8 oz	1 qt 16 oz	1 qt 24 oz	2 qt
Tomatoes, canned, whole, undrained	3 C	1 qt 16 oz	2 qt 8 oz	3 qt	4 qt	5 qt	5 qt 24 oz	6 qt 16 oz	6 qt 24 oz	2 gal
Salt	1 t	2 t	1 T	4 t	5 t	2 T	7 t	8 t	3 T	10 t
Oregano	½ t	1 t	1½ t	2 t	2½ t	1 T	3½ t	4 t	4½ t	2 T
Garlic Powder	¼ t	½ t	¾ t	1 t	1¼ t	1½ t	1¾ t	2 t	2¼ t	2½ t
Whole Kernel Corn, drained	8 oz	1 pt	1 pt 8 oz	1 qt	1 qt 8 oz	1 qt 16 oz	1 qt 24 oz	2 qt	2 qt 8 oz	2 qt 16 oz
American Cheese, cubed	4 oz	8 oz	12 oz	1 lb	1 lb 4 oz	1 lb 8 oz	1 lb 12 oz	2 lb	2 lb 4 oz	2 lb 8 oz
American Cheese, shredded	2 oz	4 oz	6 oz	8 oz	10 oz	12 oz	14 oz	1 lb	1 lb 2 oz	1 lb 4 oz

Nutrient Analysis per serving

Protein:	17 g
Carbohydrate:	15 g
Fat:	14 g
Sodium:	534 mg
Kilocalories:	259

Procedure

1. Cook spaghetti in boiling, salted water until tender; drain.
2. Brown ground beef; add celery and onion. Sauté until tender but not brown. Pour off excess fat.
3. Add tomato paste, tomatoes, and seasonings.
4. Combine hamburger mixture, spaghetti, corn, and cubed cheese.
5. Turn into baking pan or pans and sprinkle with shredded cheese.
6. Cover. Bake in 350°F oven for 50 to 60 minutes. Serve in 8 oz portions.

SPANISH BAKED STEAK

INGREDIENTS	10	20	30	40	50	60	70	80	90	100
Flour	⅓ C	⅔ C	1 C	1½ C	2 C	2⅓ C	2⅔ C	3 C	3½ C	1 qt
Salt	2 t	4 t	2 T	3 T	4 T	4½ T	5½ T	6 T	6½ T	7 T
Pepper	¼ t	½ t	1 t	1½ t	2 t	2¼ t	2½ t	3 t	3½ t	4 t
Cubed Beef Steaks, 4 oz	10	20	30	40	50	60	70	80	90	100
Vegetable Oil	2 oz	3 oz	4 oz	6 oz	1 C	10 oz	11 oz	12 oz	14 oz	2 C
Tomatoes, canned, crushed	8 oz	1 pt	1 pt 8 oz	1 qt	1 qt 16 oz	1 qt 24 oz	2 qt	2 qt 16 oz	2 qt 24 oz	3 qt
Oregano	½ t	1 t	1½ t	1 T	1½ T	4 t	5 t	2 T	2½ T	3 T
Onions	1	2	3	4	6	7	8	9	10	12

Nutrient Analysis per serving

Protein:	25 g
Carbohydrate:	4 g
Fat:	11 g
Sodium:	552 mg
Kilocalories:	234

Procedure

1. Combine flour, salt, and pepper; mix well.
2. Dredge steaks in seasoned flour; save any excess flour for use in Step 4.
3. Heat half of the vegetable oil in each of two sheet pans; arrange floured steaks in each pan; brown 10 minutes. Turn over and continue to brown another 10 minutes. Arrange steaks, shingle style, in greased steamtable pans.
4. Combine remaining flour with ½ C of juice of the tomatoes; mix until smooth. Add to tomatoes along with oregano and mix well.
5. Arrange half the onion rings over each pan of meat. Pour half of the tomato sauce over each pan of meat and onion rings. Sprinkle with paprika.
6. Cover tightly with aluminum foil and bake 1 hour until tender.

CREAMED MUSHROOM CHICKEN WITH BISCUITS

CATEGORY: *Entrée*   PORTION: ¾ C, 1 biscuit

INGREDIENTS	10	20	30	40	50	60	70	80	90	100
Chicken, cooked	1 lb 4 oz	2 lb 8 oz	3 lb 8 oz	4 lb 8 oz	6 lb	7 lb 4 oz	8 lb 8 oz	9 lb 8 oz	10 lb 8 oz	12 lb
Shortening	2 oz	4 oz	6 oz	8 oz	10 oz	12 oz	14 oz	1 lb	1 lb 2 oz	1 lb 4 oz
Flour	2 oz	4 oz	6 oz	8 oz	10 oz	12 oz	14 oz	1 lb	1 lb 2 oz	1 lb 4 oz
Chicken Broth	12 oz	1 pt 8 oz	1 qt 4 oz	1 qt 16 oz	2 qt	2 qt 12 oz	2 qt 24 oz	3 qt 4 oz	3 qt 16 oz	1 gal
Salt	½ t	1 t	1½ t	2 t	2½ t	3 t	3½ t	4 t	4½ t	5 t
Pepper	dash	⅛ t	¼ t	½ t	¾ t	1 t	1⅛ t	1¼ t	1½ t	1¾ t
Cream of Mushroom Soup	8 oz	1 pt 8 oz	2 pt	1 qt 8 oz	1 qt 16 oz	1 qt 26 oz	2 qt 8 oz	2 qt 16 oz	2 qt 24 oz	3 qt
Milk	8 oz	1 pt	1 pt 8 oz	1 pt	1 qt 8 oz	1 qt 16 oz	1 qt 24 oz	2 qt	2 qt 8 oz	2 qt 16 oz

Nutrient Analysis per serving

Protein:	20 g
Carbohydrate:	8 g
Fat:	13 g
Sodium:	521 mg
Kilocalories:	241

Procedure

1. Mix all ingredients except chicken and bring to a boil, stirring constantly.
2. Add chicken and stir together.
3. Place in 400°F oven until bubbly.
4. Remove from oven and place oven-ready biscuits on top.
5. Bake until biscuits are brown.

CHICKEN POT PIE WITH BATTER CRUST

CATEGORY: *Entrée*   PORTION: *6 oz*

INGREDIENTS	10	20	30	40	50	60	70	80	90	100
Chicken, cooked, cubed	1 lb 4 oz	2 lb 8 oz	3 lb 12 oz	5 lb	6 lb 4 oz	7 lb 8 oz	8 lb 12 oz	10 lb	11 lb 4 oz	12 lb 8 oz
Potatoes, cubed	12 oz	1 lb 8 oz	2 lb 4 oz	2 lb 12 oz	3 lb 6 oz	4 lb 4 oz	5 lb 4 oz	5 lb 8 oz	6 lb 2 oz	7 lb
Peas and Carrots	8 oz	1 lb	1 lb 8 oz	1 lb 8 oz	2 lb	2 lb 4 oz	3 lb	3 lb 4 oz	3 lb 8 oz	4 lb
Chicken Gravy	1 pt 8 oz	1 qt 16 oz	2 qt 8 oz	3 qt	1 gal	1 gal 1 qt	1 gal 3 pt	1 gal 2 qt	1 gal 3 qt	2 gal
Biscuit Mix	4 oz	8 oz	12 oz	1 lb	1 lb 4 oz	1 lb 8 oz	1 lb 12 oz	2 lb	2 lb 4 oz	2 lb 8 oz

Nutrient Analysis per serving

Protein:	18 g
Carbohydrate:	22 g
Fat:	23 g
Sodium:	954 mg
Kilocalories:	377

Procedure

1. Combine all ingredients except chicken gravy.
2. Mix in chicken gravy.
3. Prepare biscuit mix according to package directions.
4. Drop biscuit mix by the teaspoon on top of filling.
5. Bake at 350°F for 30 minutes, or until dumplings are tender.

CHICKEN AND RICE

CATEGORY: *Entrée*   PORTION: *½ C rice, 1 breast or 1 thigh & 1 leg*

INGREDIENTS	10	20	30	40	50	60	70	80	90	100
Long Grain Rice	1 lb	2 lb	3 lb	4 lb	5 lb	6 lb	7 lb	8 lb	9 lb	10 lb
Water, hot	1 pt 4 oz	2 pt 8 oz	1 qt 24 oz	2 qt 12 oz	3 qt	3 qt 16 oz	4 qt 8 oz	4 qt 24 oz	5 qt 12 oz	6 qt
Frying Chicken, cut in 8 pieces	6 lb	12 lb	18 lb	24 lb	32 lb	38 lb	44 lb	50 lb	56 lb	64 lb
Nonfat Dry Milk	4 oz	8 oz	12 oz	1 lb	1 lb 4 oz	1 lb 8 oz	2 lb	2 lb 4 oz	2 lb 8 oz	2 lb 12 oz
Water, hot	1 pt 8 oz	1 qt 16 oz	2 qt 12 oz	3 qt 6 oz	1 gal	1 gal 24 oz	1 gal 1 qt	1 gal 2 qt	1 gal 3 qt	2 gal
Chicken Base	2 oz	4 oz	6 oz	8 oz	12 oz	14 oz	1 lb	1 lb 2 oz	1 lb 4 oz	1 lb 8 oz
Butter or Margarine, melted	2 oz	4 oz	6 oz	8 oz	12 oz	14 oz	1 lb	1 lb 2 oz	1 lb 4 oz	1 lb 8 oz
Flour	4 oz	8 oz	12 oz	14 oz	1 lb	1 lb 4 oz	1 lb 8 oz	1 lb 12 oz	1 lb 14 oz	2 lb
Dry Onion Soup Mix	4 oz	8 oz	12 oz	14 oz	1 lb	1 lb 4 oz	1 lb 8 oz	1 lb 12 oz	1 lb 14 oz	2 lb

Nutrient Analysis per serving

Protein:	32 g
Carbohydrate:	17 g
Fat:	12 g
Sodium:	402 mg
Kilocalories:	319

Procedure

1. Put one-half of the rice in each of two roasting pans. Pour hot water over rice in each pan and mix.
2. Wash chicken thoroughly under running cold water. Drain well. Place one-half of the chicken evenly over the rice.
3. Stir dry milk into hot water. Add gravy base and mix well.
4. Stir melted fat and flour together until smooth. Stir into milk mixture. Cook and stir over moderate heat until thickened. Pour half of the sauce over the chicken in the roaster.
5. Pour half of the soup mix evenly over the chicken in each pan. Cover and bake 1 hour and 15 minutes at 350°F. Remove cover and bake another 30 minutes or until chicken is tender.

CHICKEN SUPREME

INGREDIENTS	10	20	30	40	50	60	70	80	90	100
Chicken Pieces	10	20	30	40	50	60	70	80	90	100
Flour, all-purpose	4 oz	8 oz	12 oz	14 oz	1 lb	1 lb 4 oz	1 lb 8 oz	1 lb 12 oz	1 lb 14 oz	2 lb
Paprika	¾ t	1½ t	2½ t	3 t	4 t	5½ t	6 t	7 t	8 t	9 t
Mushroom Soup	1 pt 4 oz	2 pt 8 oz	1 qt 24 oz	2 qt 12 oz	3 qt	3 qt 16 oz	4 qt 4 oz	4 qt 24 oz	5 qt 12 oz	6 qt
Milk	6 oz	12 oz	1 pt 4 oz	1 pt 8 oz	1 qt	1 qt 6 oz	1 qt 12 oz	1 qt 16 oz	1 qt 24 oz	2 qt

Nutrient Analysis per serving

Protein:	28 g
Carbohydrate:	13 g
Fat:	25 g
Sodium:	565 mg
Kilocalories:	401

Procedure

1. Coat chicken pieces in flour, paprika mixture.
2. Place on greased baking pan.
3. Spoon 1 T oil over each piece.
4. Bake in 350°F oven for 30 to 35 minutes or until done.
5. Remove from pan, place in 2″ deep steamtable pans.
6. Combine soup and milk in cooking pot and heat until warm; pour over chicken pieces.
7. Cover with aluminum foil and bake 30 minutes.

CHICKEN TAHITIAN

CATEGORY: *Entrée*   PORTION: *1 piece*

INGREDIENTS	10	20	30	40	50	60	70	80	90	100
Chicken, cut in 8 pieces	6 lb	13 lb	20 lb	26 lb	32 lb	39 lb	45 lb	52 lb	58 lb	65 lb
Margarine	2 oz	4 oz	6 oz	8 oz	12 oz	14 oz	1 lb	20 oz	22 oz	24 oz
Orange Juice, A.P., frozen	4 oz	8 oz	1 pt	1 pt 4 oz	1 pt 8 oz	1 pt 12 oz	1 qt	1 qt 4 oz	1 qt 8 oz	1 qt 16 oz
Margarine	4 oz	6 oz	8 oz	12 oz	1 lb	1 lb 4 oz	1 lb 6 oz	1 lb 8 oz	1 lb 12 oz	2 lb
Ginger	1 t	2 t	3 t	4 t	6 t	7 t	8 t	9 t	10 t	11 t
Soy Sauce	1 t	2 t	3 t	4 t	6 t	7 t	8 t	9 t	10 t	11 t

Nutrient Analysis per serving

Protein:	29 g
Carbohydrate:	1 g
Fat:	21 g
Sodium:	262 mg
Kilocalories:	321

Procedure

1. Melt fat in baking pans. Arrange chicken in pans in a single layer. Brown in the oven.
2. Combine juice, margarine, ginger, and soy sauce. Brush chicken with the orange mixture.
3. Bake 325°F for 1 hour.
4. Baste with orange mixture until the chicken is glazed.

CRISPY BAKED CHICKEN

CATEGORY: *Entrée*   PORTION: *3 to 4 oz*

INGREDIENTS	10	20	30	40	50	60	70	80	90	100
Chicken, cut in 8 pieces	6 lb	13 lb	20 lb	26 lb	32 lb	39 lb	45 lb	52 lb	58 lb	65 lb
Salad Dressing, light	1 pt	1 qt	1 qt 16 oz	2 qt	2 qt 16 oz	3 qt	3 qt 16 oz	4 qt	4 qt 16 oz	5 qt
Cornflake Crumbs	1 pt	1 qt	1 qt 16 oz	2 qt	2 qt 16 oz	3 qt	3 qt 16 oz	4 qt	4 qt 16 oz	5 qt
Parmesan Cheese, grated	8 oz	1 lb	1 lb 8 oz	2 lb	2 lb 8 oz	3 lb	3 lb 8 oz	4 lb	4 lb 8 oz	5 lb
Salt and Pepper	dash	¼ t	½ t	¾ t	1 t	1¼ t	1½ t	1¾ t	2 t	2½ t

Nutrient Analysis per serving

Protein:	38 g
Carbohydrate:	31 g
Fat:	21 g
Sodium:	901 mg
Kilocalories:	481

Procedure

1. Brush chicken with salad dressing.
2. Coat with combined remaining ingredients.
3. Place in greased pan and bake uncovered for 1 hour or until done at 350°F.

CRUSTY OVEN-BAKED CHICKEN

CATEGORY: Entrée   *PORTION: 4 oz breast*

INGREDIENTS	10	20	30	40	50	60	70	80	90	100
Corn Flake Crumbs	1 C	2 C	3 C	4 C	5 C	6 C	7 C	8 C	9 C	10 C
Salt	1½ t	3 t	1½ T	2 T	2½ T	3 T	3½ T	4 T	4½ T	5 T
Pepper	¼ t	½ t	¾ t	1 t	1¼ t	1½ t	1¾ t	2 t	2¼ t	2½ t
Paprika	1 t	2 t	3 t	4 t	5 t	6 t	7 t	8 t	9 t	10 t
Garlic Salt	½ t	1 t	1½ t	2 t	2½ t	3 t	3½ t	4 t	4½ t	5 t
Onion Salt	½ t	1 t	1½ t	2 t	2½ t	3 t	3½ t	4 t	4½ t	5 t
Egg	2	4	6	8	10	12	14	16	18	20
Lemon Juice	2 t	1 T	1½ T	2 T	2½ T	3 T	3½ T	4 T	4½ T	5 T
Chicken Breasts	10	20	30	40	50	60	70	80	90	100

Nutrient Analysis per serving

Protein:	29 g
Carbohydrate:	5 g
Fat:	7 g
Sodium:	479 mg
Kilocalories:	218

Procedure

1. Combine crumbs, salt, pepper, paprika, garlic salt, and onion salt.
2. In a shallow bowl combine egg and lemon juice; beat slightly.
3. Dip chicken in egg mixture; coat with crumb mixture.
4. Place on ungreased baking pan.
5. Bake uncovered at 350°F for 1 to 1¼ hours until chicken is done.

CURRIED CHICKEN WITH BROCCOLI

CATEGORY: Entrée   *PORTION: 6 oz*

INGREDIENTS	10	20	30	40	50	60	70	80	90	100
Chicken, cooked and diced	1 lb 8 oz	3 lb	4 lb 8 oz	6 lb	7 lb 8 oz	9 lb	10 lb 8 oz	12 lb	13 lb 8 oz	15 lb
Broccoli Spears, cooked	1 lb 4 oz	2 lb 8 oz	3 lb 12 oz	5 lb	6 lb 4 oz	7 lb	8 lb 12 oz	10 lb	11 lb 4 oz	12 lb 8 oz
Canned Cream of Chicken Soup (undiluted)	1 pt 4 oz	2 pt 8 oz	3 pt 12 oz	1 gal 16 oz	1 gal 1 qt	1 gal 3 pt	2 gal	2 gal 1 pt	2 gal 2 pt	2 gal 2 qt
Mayonnaise	8 oz	1 pt	1 pt 8 oz	1 qt	1 qt 8 oz	1 qt 16 oz	1 qt 24 oz	2 qt	2 qt 8 oz	2 qt 16 oz
Curry Powder	2 t	1 T	2 T	2½ T	3 T	4 T	4½ T	5 T	5½ T	6 T
American Cheese, shredded	8 oz	1 lb	1 lb 8 oz	2 lb	2 lb 8 oz	3 lb	3 lb 8 oz	4 lb	4 lb 8 oz	5 lb

Nutrient Analysis per serving

Protein:	27 g
Carbohydrate:	6 g
Fat:	29 g
Sodium:	536 mg
Kilocalories:	399

Procedure

1. Place cooked broccoli spears on the bottom of a greased baking pan. Top with chicken.
2. Combine soup, mayonnaise, curry, and cheese. Mix well. Spread mixture over chicken and broccoli.
3. Bake in 350°F oven until bubbly, about 35 to 40 minutes.

HONEYED CHICKEN—CHINESE STYLE

CATEGORY: Entrée　　*PORTION: 1 piece*

INGREDIENTS	10	20	30	40	50	60	70	80	90	100
Frying Chicken, cut in 8 pieces	5 lb	10 lb	14 lb	20 lb	24 lb	29 lb	34 lb	38 lb	44 lb	48 lb
Eggs	2	3	5	6	7	10	11	13	14	16
Margarine, melted	2 oz	3 oz	4 oz	6 oz	8 oz	10 oz	11 oz	12 oz	14 oz	1 lb
Lemon Juice	2 oz	3 oz	4 oz	6 oz	8 oz	10 oz	11 oz	12 oz	14 oz	1 pt
Honey	4 oz	6 oz	8 oz	12 oz	1 pt	1 pt 4 oz	1 pt 6 oz	1 pt 8 oz	1 pt 12 oz	1 qt
Soy Sauce	1½ T	2½ T	¼ C	⅓ C	½ C	½ C	⅔ C	⅔ C	¾ C	1 C

Nutrient Analysis per serving

Protein:	30 g
Carbohydrate:	14 g
Fat:	13 g
Sodium:	291 mg
Kilocalories:	303

Procedure

1. Place chicken pieces in shallow baking pans.
2. Beat eggs slightly.
3. Add melted margarine, soy sauce, lemon juice, and honey to eggs and mix well.
4. Pour sauce over chicken, turning pieces to coat.
5. Bake uncovered in oven at 300°F for 1 hour or until done.

INGREDIENTS	10	20	30	40	50	60	70	80	90	100
Chickens, portions	10	20	30	40	50	60	70	80	90	100
Oil	¼ C	½ C	1 C	1½ C	2 C	2¼ C	2½ C	3 C	3½ C	4 C
Salt	1½ t	2 t	1 T	1½ T	2 T	2½ T	3 T	3½ T	4 T	4½ T
Onion Powder	⅛ t	¼ t	½ t	¾ t	1 t	1⅛ t	1¼ t	1½ t	1¾ t	2 t
Red Pepper, ground	⅛ t	¼ t	½ t	¾ t	1 t	1⅛ t	1¼ t	1½ t	1¾ t	2 t
Mustard, powdered	2 T	¼ C	⅓ C	½ C	⅔ C	¾ C	¾ C 2 T	1 C	1 C 2 T	1¼ C
Water, warm	1 T	2 T	¼ C	⅓ C	½ C	½ C	1 T ½ C	2 T ¾ C	¾ C 1 T	1 C
Margarine, melted	2 oz	4 oz	6 oz	8 oz	10 oz	12 oz	14 oz	1 lb	1 lb 2 oz	1 lb 4 oz
White Wine, dry	2 T	¼ C	½ C	¾ C	1 C	1 C 2 T	1¼ C	1½ C	1¾ C	2 C
Lemon Juice	1 T	2 T	3 T	¼ C	⅓ C	⅓ C	2 T ½ C	⅔ C	¾ C	1 C
Bread Crumbs, dry	12 oz	1 pt 8 oz	1 qt 4 oz	1 qt 1 pt	2 qt	2 pt 12 oz	2 qt 24 oz	3 qt 4 oz	3 qt 1 pt	4 qt

Nutrient Analysis per serving

Protein:	33 g
Carbohydrate:	3 g
Fat:	22 g
Sodium:	416 mg
Kilocalories:	358

Procedure

1. Mix together oil, salt, onion powder, and pepper; dip chicken in oil. Place in shallow pan and bake at 375°F until tender, about 35 minutes.
2. Mix mustard with water; let stand 10 minutes. Add butter, wine, and lemon juice. Mix well.
3. Brush baked chicken with mustard mixture; coat with bread crumbs.
4. Place chicken on rack in broiler pans. Broil 6 inches from heat until browned, about 2 minutes on each side.

OLD-FASHIONED CHICKEN AND NOODLES

CATEGORY: Entrée   PORTION: 1 C

INGREDIENTS	10	20	30	40	50	60	70	80	90	100
Noodles	4 oz	8 oz	12 oz	1 lb	1 lb 4 oz	1 lb 8 oz	1 lb 12 oz	2 lb	2 lb 4 oz	2 lb 8 oz
Chicken Stock	24 oz	1 qt 16 oz	2 qt 12 oz	3 qt	1 gal	1 gal 24 oz	1 gal ½ qt	1 gal 2½ qt	1 gal 3 qt	2 gal
Chicken, cooked, boned	2 lb	4 lb	6 lb	8 lb	10 lb	12 lb	14 lb	16 lb	18 lb	20 lb
Margarine	1 oz	2 oz	3 oz	4 oz	5 oz	6 oz	7 oz	8 oz	9 oz	10 oz
Flour	1 T	2 T	3 T	4 T	5 T	6 T	7 T	8 T	9 T	10 T
Chicken Stock or Milk	8 oz	1 pt 4 oz	1 pt 14 oz	2 pt 8 oz	1 qt 16 oz	1 qt 24 oz	2 qt 4 oz	2 qt 16 oz	2 qt 24 oz	3 qt
Salt	¼ t	½ t	¾ t	1 t	1½ t	1¾ t	2 t	2¼ t	2½ t	3 t
Pepper	⅛ t	¼ t	½ t	¾ t	1 t	1⅛ t	1¼ t	1½ t	1¾ t	2 t

Nutrient Analysis per serving

Protein:	30 g
Carbohydrate:	7 g
Fat:	7 g
Sodium:	411 mg
Kilocalories:	229

Procedure

1. Heat chicken stock to boiling, add noodles and cook 20 minutes.
2. Remove noodles from pan; drain, and place in greased baking pan.
3. Add cooked chicken to the noodles.
4. Make sauce of flour, stock, margarine, milk, salt, and pepper.
5. Pour over chicken and noodles.
6. Bake at 350°F for 30 minutes.

TANGY BAKED CHICKEN

CATEGORY: *Entrée*   PORTION: *1 piece*

INGREDIENTS	10	20	30	40	50	60	70	80	90	100
Chicken Breast, halves	10	20	30	40	50	60	70	80	90	100
Bread Crumbs, fine	6 oz	12 oz	1 lb 4 oz	1 lb 8 oz	2 lb	2 lb 6 oz	2 lb 12 oz	3 lb 4 oz	3 lb 8 oz	4 lb
French Dressing	4 oz	8 oz	12 oz	14 oz	1 pt 2 oz	1 pt 6 oz	1 pt 10 oz	1 pt 14 oz	2 pt	2 pt 4 oz

Nutrient Analysis per serving

Protein:	31 g
Carbohydrate:	14 g
Fat:	13 g
Sodium:	347 mg
Kilocalories:	307

Procedure

1. Place bread crumbs in shallow dish.
2. Coat chicken with French dressing and dip in bread crumbs.
3. Bake uncovered for 1 hour in 350°F oven.

TURKEY PIE WITH CORNBREAD TOPPING

CATEGORY: *Entrée*   PORTION: *8 oz*

INGREDIENTS	10	20	30	40	50	60	70	80	90	100
Margarine	1 oz	2 oz	3 oz	4 oz	5 oz	6 oz	7 oz	8 oz	9 oz	10 oz
Onions, chopped	2 oz	4 oz	6 oz	8 oz	10 oz	12 oz	14 oz	1 lb	1 lb 2 oz	1 lb 4 oz
Mushrooms, sliced	10 oz	1 lb 4 oz	1 lb 14 oz	2 lb 8 oz	3 lb	3 lb 10 oz	4 lb 4 oz	4 lb 14 oz	5 lb 8 oz	6 lb
Lemon Juice	1 oz	2 oz	3 oz	4 oz	5 oz	6 oz	7 oz	8 oz	9 oz	10 oz
Sherry	2 oz	4 oz	6 oz	1 C	1 C 2 oz	1¼ C	1 C 6 oz	2 C	2 C 2 oz	2 C 4 oz
Turkey, cooked, diced	1 lb 10 oz	3 lb 4 oz	4 lb 14 oz	6 lb 8 oz	8 lb	9 lb 10 oz	11 lb 4 oz	12 lb 14 oz	14 lb 8 oz	16 lb
Velouté Sauce (*see* recipe)	1 qt 16 oz	3 qt	1 gal 16 oz	1 gal 2 qt	2 gal	2 gal 1 qt	2 gal 3 qt	3 gal 16 oz	3 gal 2 qt	4 gal
Salt	½ t	1 t	1½ t	2 t	2½ t	3 t	3½ t	4 t	4½ t	5 t
Pepper	¼ t	½ t	¾ t	1 t	1¼ t	1½ t	1¾ t	2 t	2¼ t	2½ t
Pimiento, diced	¼ C	½ C	¾ C	1 C	1¼ C	1½ C	1¾ C	2 C	2¼ C	2½ C
Cornbread Topping (*see* recipe)										

Nutrient Analysis per serving

Protein:	25 g
Carbohydrate:	28 g
Fat:	18 g
Sodium:	476 mg
Kilocalories:	390

Procedure

1. Melt butter. Add onions and sauté until transparent.
2. Add mushrooms and lemon juice; cook until tender.
3. Add sherry wine; reduce to one-half.
4. Add turkey and heat thoroughly. Add white sauce and bring to boil. Add pimiento last.
5. Ladle into baking pan.
6. Top with cornbread topping. (*See* recipe.) Bake in 400°F oven for 40 minutes or until topping is lightly browned.

CHEESE CASSEROLE

CATEGORY: *Entrée*   PORTION: *6 oz*

INGREDIENTS	10	20	30	40	50	60	70	80	90	100
Bread	1 lb	1 lb 8 oz	2 lb	2 lb 8 oz	3 lb	4 lb	4 lb 8 oz	5 lb	5 lb 8 oz	6 lb
Cheese, sliced	8 oz	1 lb	1 lb 8 oz	2 lb	2 lb 8 oz	3 lb	3 lb 8 oz	4 lb	4 lb 8 oz	5 lb
Margarine	4 oz	8 oz	12 oz	1 lb	1 lb 4 oz	1 lb 8 oz	1 lb 12 oz	2 lb	2 lb 4 oz	2 lb 8 oz
Milk	2½ C	1 qt	1 qt 8 oz	2 qt	2 qt 8 oz	3 qt	3 qt 8 oz	4 qt	4 qt 8 oz	5 qt
Eggs, well-beaten	8	16	24	32	42	50	58	66	74	84
Mustard, prepared	½ t	1 t	1½ t	2 t	2½ t	3 t	3½ t	4 t	4½ t	5 t
Tabasco	⅛ t	¼ t	¼ t	½ t	½ t	¾ t	¾ t	1 t	1 t	1⅛ t

Nutrient Analysis per serving

Protein:	16 g
Carbohydrate:	13 g
Fat:	21 g
Sodium:	644 mg
Kilocalories:	319

Procedure

1. Spread bread or toast with margarine and make cheese sandwiches in the bottom of a sheet pan.
2. Combine eggs and milk, add tabasco and mustard. Pour over bread and cheese. Let stand at least 3 hours in refrigerator.
3. Bake at 325°F for 1 hour. May be served with strips of bacon on top.

BAKED FISH PARISIENNE

INGREDIENTS	10	20	30	40	50	60	70	80	90	100
White Fish, 4 oz	10	20	30	40	50	60	70	80	90	100
French Dressing	4 oz	8 oz	12 oz	14 oz	1 pt 2 oz	1 pt 6 oz	1 pt 10 oz	1 pt 14 oz	2 qt	2 pt 4 oz
French-fried Onions, canned	4 oz	8 oz	12 oz	14 oz	1 lb 2 oz	1 lb 6 oz	1 lb 10 oz	1 lb 14 oz	2 lb	2 lb 4 oz

Nutrient Analysis per serving

Procedure

Protein:	18 g
Carbohydrate:	17 g
Fat:	25 g
Sodium:	511 mg
Kilocalories:	375

1. Mix French dressing with onions.
2. Pour over white fish and bake in 350°F oven for 15 to 20 minutes.

OVEN-BROILED FISH FILLETS

CATEGORY: *Entrée*   PORTION: *3 oz*

INGREDIENTS	10	20	30	40	50	60	70	80	90	100
Halibut Fish Fillet	1 lb 4 oz	2 lb 8 oz	3 lb 12 oz	5 lb	6 lb 4 oz	7 lb 8 oz	8 lb 12 oz	10 lb	11 lb 4 oz	12 lb 8 oz
Salt	1½ t	3 t	4½ t	2 T	3 T	3½ T	4 T	5 T	6 T	7 T
Pepper, black, ground	½ t	1 t	1¼ t	1½ t	2 t	2½ t	3 t	3¼ t	3½ t	4 t
Paprika, ground	¾ t	1½ t	2¼ t	3 t	3¾ t	4½ t	5¼ t	6 t	6¾ t	7½ t
Margarine, melted	2 oz	4 oz	8 oz	10 oz	12 oz	14 oz	1 lb	1 lb 4 oz	1 lb 6 oz	1 lb 8 oz
Lemon Juice	¼ C	⅓ C	½ C	¾ C	1 C	1¼ C	1⅓ C	1½ C	1¾ C	2 C

Nutrient Analysis per serving

Protein:	14 g
Carbohydrate:	.7 g
Fat:	5 g
Sodium:	194 mg
Kilocalories:	99

Procedure

1. Place fish portions on well-greased sheet pans.
2. Combine remaining ingredients. Pour evenly over fish.
3. Bake in 425°F oven for 15 minutes or until slightly browned.
4. Garnish each portion with chopped parsley and a thin slice of lemon.

TUNA MELT

CATEGORY: Entrée   PORTION: 1

INGREDIENTS	10	20	30	40	50	60	70	80	90	100
Tuna, packed in water	12 oz	1 lb 10 oz	2 lb 8 oz	3 lb 4 oz	4 lb 2 oz	5 lb	5 lb 12 oz	6 lb 8 oz	7 lb 6 oz	8 lb 6 oz
Onion, finely chopped	1 oz	2 oz	3 oz	4 oz	4 oz	5 oz	6 oz	7 oz	7 oz	8 oz
Green Pepper, finely chopped	1 oz	2 oz	3 oz	4 oz	4 oz	6 oz	7 oz	8 oz	9 oz	10 oz
Celery, finely chopped	½ C	1 C	1½ C	1¾ C	2 C	2½ C	3 C	3½ C	3¾ C	4 C
Pickle Relish, well-drained	½ C	1 C	1½ C	1¾ C	2 C	2½ C	3 C	3½ C	3¾ C	4 C
Mayonnaise	6 oz	12 oz	1 pt 2 oz	1 pt 8 oz	1 qt	1 qt 6 oz	1 qt 12 oz	1 qt 18 oz	1 qt 24 oz	2 qt
Toast	10	20	30	40	50	60	70	80	90	100
Tomatoes, cut 6 slices	1½	3	4½	6	8	9½	11	12½	14	16
American or Swiss Cheese Slices	10	20	30	40	50	60	70	80	90	100

Nutrient Analysis per serving

Protein:	17 g
Carbohydrate:	20 g
Fat:	21 g
Sodium:	949 mg
Kilocalories:	348

Procedure

1. Drain and flake tuna.
2. Gently mix tuna with other ingredients. Keep chilled.
3. Place #16 scoop of tuna salad on toast.
4. Top with one slice tomato and slice of cheese.
5. Broil until cheese melts.

Entrées   107

BACON-WRAPPED FRANKS

CATEGORY: *Entrée*   PORTION: 1

INGREDIENTS	10	20	30	40	50	60	70	80	90	100
Bacon	6 oz	12 oz	1 lb 4 oz	1 lb 8 oz	2 lb	2 lb 6 oz	2 lb 12 oz	3 lb 4 oz	3 lb 8 oz	4 lb
Frankfurters, 8 per lb	10	20	30	40	50	60	70	80	90	100
American Cheese, 1 oz slices	4 oz	8 oz	12 oz	1 lb	1 lb 8 oz	1 lb 12 oz	2 lb	2 lb 4 oz	2 lb 8 oz	3 lb 2 oz

Nutrient Analysis per serving

Protein:	10 g
Carbohydrate:	1 g
Fat:	23 g
Sodium:	905 mg
Kilocalories:	260

Procedure

1. Cut bacon strips in half and partially cook, not crisp.
2. Cut a lengthwise slit in each frankfurter. Make sure not to cut all the way through.
3. Cut 1 oz slices of cheese into fourths.
4. Stuff each frankfurter with ¼ oz American cheese.
5. Wrap ½ slice of partially cooked bacon around frankfurter and secure with a toothpick.
6. Place on a sheet pan and bake at 425°F for 10 minutes until bacon is crisp and cheese melts.

BAKED HAM SLICES

INGREDIENTS	10	20	30	40	50	60	70	80	90	100
Ham	3 lb	6 lb	9 lb	12 lb	15 lb	18 lb	21 lb	24 lb	27 lb	30 lb
Brown Sugar	2 oz	3 oz	4 oz	6 oz	8 oz	10 oz	11 oz	12 oz	14 oz	1 lb
Fruit Juice	1 oz	2 oz	3 oz	4 oz	5 oz	6 oz	7 oz	8 oz	10 oz	12 oz

Nutrient Analysis per serving

Protein:	16 g
Carbohydrate:	6 g
Fat:	6 g
Sodium:	1091 mg
Kilocalories:	156

Procedure

1. Place ham slices in baking pans.
2. Combine juice and brown sugar and pour over ham.
3. Bake at 325°F for 1 hour.

BARBECUED FRANKS

CATEGORY: Entrée   *PORTION: 2 franks*

INGREDIENTS	10	20	30	40	50	60	70	80	90	100
Onions, finely chopped	¾ C	1½ C	2¼ C	3 C	1 qt	1 qt ¾ C	1 qt 1½ C	1 qt 2¼ C	1 qt 3 C	2 qt
Celery, chopped	¾ C	1½ C	2¼ C	3 C	1 qt	1 qt ¾ C	1 qt 1½ C	1 qt 2¼ C	1 qt 3 C	2 qt
Garlic, minced	½ clove	½ clove	½ clove	1 clove	1 clove	1 clove	1 clove	1½ clove	1½ clove	2 cloves
Shortening	2 oz	4 oz	6 oz	8 oz	10 oz	12 oz	14 oz	1 lb	1 lb 2 oz	1 lb 4 oz
Barbecue Sauce, all-purpose	12 oz	1 pt 8 oz	1 qt 4 oz	1 qt 16 oz	2 qt	2 qt 12 oz	2 qt 24 oz	3 qt 4 oz	3 qt 16 oz	1 gal
Water	¾ C	1½ C	2¼ C	3 C	1 qt	1 qt 6 oz	1 qt 12 oz	1 qt 16 oz	1 qt 24 oz	2 qt
Frankfurters, scored	20	20	60	80	100	120	140	160	180	200

Nutrient Analysis per serving

Protein:	10 g
Carbohydrate:	8 g
Fat:	31 g
Sodium:	1298 mg
Kilocalories:	362

Procedure

1. Brown onions, celery, and garlic in shortening.
2. Add barbecue sauce and water, stirring well. Add frankfurters.
3. Cover; simmer 10 minutes.
4. Serve two franks per portion.

BOILED DINNER

CATEGORY: *Entrée*   PORTION: *2 oz ham, ¾ C vegetable*

INGREDIENTS	10	20	30	40	50	60	70	80	90	100
Ham, cubed	1 lb 8 oz	3 lb	4 lb 8 oz	6 lb	8 lb	9 lb 8 oz	11 lb	12 lb 8 oz	14 lb	16 lb
Potatoes, cubed	1 qt	2 qt	3 qt	4 qt	5 qt	6 qt	7 qt	8 qt	9 qt	10 qt
Turnips, cubed	1 qt	2 qt	3 qt	4 qt	5 qt	6 qt	7 qt	8 qt	9 qt	10 qt
Cabbage, wedges	1 qt	2 qt	3 qt	4 qt	5 qt	6 qt	7 qt	8 qt	9 qt	10 qt
Carrots, sliced	1 qt	2 qt	3 qt	4 qt	5 qt	6 qt	7 qt	8 qt	9 qt	10 qt

Nutrient Analysis per serving

Protein:	14 g
Carbohydrate:	20 g
Fat:	11 g
Sodium:	761 mg
Kilocalories:	233 mg

Procedure

1. Heat ham in covered pan in oven.
2. Parboil the potatoes.
3. Cook turnips, carrots, and cabbage in ham juice and water until tender. *Do Not Overcook.*
4. Mix potatoes and other vegetables together.
5. Serve ¾ C vegetable with 2 oz ham per serving.

COUNTRY SAUSAGE BURGER

CATEGORY: Entrée   PORTION: 1 biscuit, 1 patty

INGREDIENTS	10	20	30	40	50	60	70	80	90	100
Bulk Sausage	2 lb 8 oz	5 lb	7 lb 8 oz	10 lb	12 lb 8 oz	15 lb	15 lb 8 oz	20 lb	22 lb 8 oz	25 lb
Buttermilk Biscuit:										
Flour, all-purpose	8 oz	1 lb	1 lb 8 oz	2 lb	2 lb 8 oz	3 lb	3 lb 8 oz	4 lb	4 lb 8 oz	5 lb
Baking Powder	½ oz	1 oz	1½ oz	2 oz	2½ oz	3 oz	3½ oz	4 oz	4½ oz	5 oz
Baking Soda	¼ t	½ t	¾ t	1 t	1½ t	1¼ t	2 t	2¼ t	2½ t	1 T
Salt	½ t	1 t	1½ t	2 t	3 t	3½ t	4 t	4½ t	5 t	2 T
Shortening, hydrogenated	2 oz	4 oz	6 oz	8 oz	10 oz	12 oz	14 oz	1 lb	1 lb 2 oz	1 lb 4 oz
Buttermilk	4 oz	8 oz	12 oz	1 pt	24 oz	28 oz	1 qt	1 qt 4 oz	1 qt 8 oz	1 qt 24 oz

Nutrient Analysis per serving

Protein:	14 g
Carbohydrate:	18 g
Fat:	32 g
Sodium:	1039 mg
Kilocalories:	420

Procedure

1. Form sausage into 4 oz patty and bake in oven until done. Drain well.
2. For biscuits, combine dry ingredients in mixer bowl. Blend on low speed, using flat beater, for 10 seconds.
3. Add shortening to flour mixture. Mix on low speed for 1 minute. Scrape sides and bottom of bowl. Mix 1 minute longer. Mixture will be crumbly.
4. Add milk. Mix on low speed to form a soft dough, about 30 seconds.
5. Roll dough to ¾" thickness. Cut with a 2½" cutter and bake at 425°F for 15 minutes or until golden brown.
6. Serve 2 oz sausage burger between halved biscuit.

HAM LOAF

INGREDIENTS	10	20	30	40	50	60	70	80	90	100
Ham, ground	1 lb 4 oz	2 lb	3 lb	4 lb	5 lb	6 lb	7 lb	8 lb	9 lb	10 lb
Beef, ground	8 oz	1 lb	1 lb 8 oz	2 lb	2 lb 8 oz	3 lb	3 lb 8 oz	4 lb	4 lb 8 oz	5 lb
Pork, ground	8 oz	1 lb	1 lb 8 oz	2 lb	2 lb 8 oz	3 lb	3 lb 8 oz	4 lb	4 lb 8 oz	5 lb
Bread Crumbs	8 oz	16 oz	24 oz	1 qt	1 qt 8 oz	1 qt 16 oz	1 qt 24 oz	2 qt	2 qt 8 oz	2 qt 16 oz
Milk	½ C	1 C	1½ C	2½ C	3 C	3¾ C	4 C	5 C	6 C	6¼ C
Eggs	2	4	6	7	10	12	14	16	18	20
Mustard, dry	⅛ t	¼ t	⅓ t	½ t	⅔ t	¾ t	¾ t	1 t	1⅛ t	1¼ t
Glaze for Ham Loaf (*see* recipe, p. 188)										

Nutrient Analysis per serving

Protein:	13 g
Carbohydrate:	14 g
Fat:	14 g
Sodium:	326 mg
Kilocalories:	247

Procedure

1. Oil pans.
2. Mix bread crumbs, dry mustard, milk, and eggs.
3. Combine meat and mix with other ingredients. *Do Not Overmix.*
4. Make into loaves, 1 qt each.
5. Bake at 350°F for 1 to 1½ hours.
6. Remove from oven last 12 minutes of baking and brush with glaze (*see* recipe for Glaze).

HUNGARIAN-STYLE PORK CUTLET

CATEGORY: *Entrée*   PORTION: *3 oz*

INGREDIENTS	10	20	30	40	50	60	70	80	90	100
Pork Cutlet, 4 oz portion	10	20	30	40	50	60	70	80	90	100
Flour	2 oz	4 oz	6 oz	8 oz	12 oz	14 oz	1 lb	1 lb 2 oz	1 lb 4 oz	1 lb 8 oz
Salt	1 t	2 t	3 t	4 t	2 T	2¼ T	2½ T	3 T	3½ T	4 T
Pepper, white	⅛ t	¼ t	½ t	¾ t	1 t	1⅛ t	1¼ t	1½ t	1¾ t	2 t
Cream of Mushroom Soup	16 oz	1 qt	1 qt 16 oz	2 qt 12 oz	3 qt	3 qt 16 oz	4 qt	4 qt 16 oz	5 qt	6 qt
Water	4 oz	6 oz	8 oz	12 oz	1 pt	1 pt 4 oz	1 pt 6 oz	1 pt 8 oz	1 pt 12 oz	1 qt
Thyme	½ t	1 t	1½ t	1¾ t	2 t	2½ t	3 t	3½ t	3¾ t	4 t
Dehydrated Onions	1½ t	1 T	1½ T	2 T	3 T	¼ C	⅓ C	½ C	¾ C	1 C
Parsley, chopped	2 oz	6 oz	8 oz	12 oz	1 pt	1 pt 2 oz	1 pt 6 oz	1 pt 8 oz	1 pt 12 oz	1 qt
Sour Cream	2 oz	6 oz	8 oz	12 oz	1 pt	1 pt 2 oz	1 pt 6 oz	1 pt 8 oz	1 pt 12 oz	1 qt

Nutrient Analysis per serving

Protein:	20 g
Carbohydrate:	8 g
Fat:	31 g
Sodium:	653 mg
Kilocalories:	408

Procedure

1. Mix flour, salt, and white pepper together.
2. Flour each cutlet and brown.
3. Arrange on sheet pans.
4. Blend together soup, water, and thyme. Heat thoroughly.
5. Add parsley and sour cream and mix well.
6. Stir in onions.
7. Divide sauce equally to each pan of cutlets.
8. Cover and bake at 350°F for 1 hour.

OVEN-BAKED PORK CHOP WITH DRESSING

CATEGORY: Entrée   PORTION: 1 chop with ⅓ C dressing

INGREDIENTS	10	20	30	40	50	60	70	80	90	100
Pork Chops, 4 oz	10	20	30	40	50	60	70	80	90	100
Bread Crumbs, dry	8 oz	1 lb	1 lb 8 oz	2 lb	2 lb 8 oz	3 lb	3 lb 8 oz	4 lb	4 lb 8 oz	5 lb
Margarine, melted	2 oz	2 oz	3 oz	3 oz	4 oz	4 oz	5 oz	6 oz	7 oz	8 oz
Onions, chopped	½ C	1 C	1½ C	1¾ C	2 C	2½ C	2¾ C	3 C	3½ C	1 qt
Poultry Seasoning	½ t	1 t	1½ t	2 t	3 t	3½ t	4 t	4½ t	5 t	6 t
Salt	⅛ t	¼ t	½ t	¾ t	1 t	1⅛ t	1¼ t	1½ t	1¾ t	2 t
Eggs, beaten	1	1	2	2	3	3	4	4	5	6
Water, warm	8 oz	1 pt 4 oz	1 pt 12 oz	1 qt	1 qt 16 oz	1 qt 24 oz	2 qt 2 oz	2 qt 12 oz	2 qt 16 oz	3 qt

Nutrient Analysis per serving

Protein:	21 g
Carbohydrate:	12 g
Fat:	33 g
Sodium:	257 mg
Kilocalories:	441

Procedure

1. Put chops on lightly greased sheet pans; bake 1 hour; pour off as much fat as possible.
2. Combine bread, margarine, onions, poultry seasoning, and salt. Mix lightly. Add eggs and warm water and mix lightly.
3. Put ¼ C dressing on top of each chop.
4. Pour enough water in each pan to cover bottom of pan about ⅛" deep.
5. Bake 1 to 1½ hours or until chops are tender and dressing is lightly browned.

OVEN-FRIED PORK CHOP

INGREDIENTS	10	20	30	40	50	60	70	80	90	100
Pork Chops, 4 oz	2 lb 8 oz	5 lb	7 lb 8 oz	10 lb	12 lb 8 oz	15 lb	17 lb 8 oz	20 lb	22 lb 8 oz	25 lb
Flour	3 T	2 oz	4 oz	6 oz	8 oz	9 oz	10 oz	12 oz	14 oz	1 lb
Salt	1 t	2 t	3 t	4 t	5 t	6 t	7 t	8 t	9 t	10 t

Nutrient Analysis per serving

Protein:	23 g
Carbohydrate:	3 g
Fat:	12 g
Sodium:	177 mg
Kilocalories:	225

Procedure

1. Dredge chops in flour and salt mixture.
2. Sauté in small amount of fat until brown on both sides.
3. Place on well-greased sheet pans.
4. Cover and bake in 350°F oven 1 hour.

PORK CUTLETS SUPREME

INGREDIENTS	10	20	30	40	50	60	70	80	90	100
Onion, sliced thin	8 oz	1 lb	1 lb 8 oz	2 lb	2 lb 8 oz	3 lb	3 lb 8 oz	4 lb	4 lb 8 oz	5 lb
Lemon Slices	10	20	30	40	50	60	70	80	90	100
Brown Sugar	4 oz	8 oz	12 oz	1 lb	1 lb 4 oz	1 lb 8 oz	1 lb 16 oz	2 lb	2 lb 4 oz	2 lb 8 oz
Ketchup	4 oz	8 oz	12 oz	1 pt	1 pt 4 oz	1 pt 8 oz	1 pt 12 oz	1 qt	1 qt 4 oz	1 qt 8 oz
Pork Cutlets, 4 oz	10	20	30	40	50	60	70	80	90	100

Nutrient Analysis per serving

Protein:	19 g
Carbohydrate:	16 g
Fat:	27 g
Sodium:	189 mg
Kilocalories:	392

Procedure

1. Arrange cutlets on baking pan.
2. Top each cutlet with one thin slice onion, a slice of lemon, 1 T brown sugar, and 1 T ketchup.
3. Cover and bake at 350°F for 45 minutes.
4. Uncover and bake 30 minutes.
5. Baste before serving.

HOT HAM AND CHEESE SANDWICH

INGREDIENTS	10	20	30	40	50	60	70	80	90	100
Ham, ground	10 oz	1 lb 4 oz	1 lb 12 oz	2 lb 8 oz	3 lb 2 oz	3 lb 12 oz	4 lb 6 oz	5 lb	5 lb 10 oz	6 lb 4 oz
Mustard, prepared	1 oz	2 oz	3 oz	4 oz	5 oz	6 oz	7 oz	8 oz	9 oz	10 oz
Pickle Relish	½ C	1 C	1½ C	2 C	2½ C	3 C	3½ C	4 C	4½ C	5 C
Process Cheese, grated	10 oz	1 lb 4 oz	1 lb 12 oz	2 lb 8 oz	3 lb 2 oz	3 lb 12 oz	4 lb 6 oz	5 lb	5 lb 8 oz	6 lb 4 oz
Mayonnaise or Salad Dressing	¼ C	½ C	¾ C	1 C	1¼ C	1½ C	1¾ C	2 C	2¼ C	2½ C
Sandwich Buns, sliced	10	20	30	40	50	60	70	80	90	100

Nutrient Analysis per serving

Protein:	16 g
Carbohydrate:	27 g
Fat:	19 g
Sodium:	1096 mg
Kilocalories:	351

Procedure

1. Combine ham, mustard, pickle relish, cheese, and mayonnaise. Mix well.
2. Place both halves of buns on pan, cut sides up, arranging so all tops are facing the same direction.
3. Place #12 scoop of filling on bottom half of each sliced bun. Turn scoop over and mash filling down with back of scoop before dipping up another scoopful for the next bun.
4. Heat as needed in 350°F oven (about 8 to 10 minutes) until bun tops toast and cheese melts.

CHAPTER 6 *Vegetables and Starch Dishes*

BEETS WITH PINEAPPLE

CATEGORY: Vegetable   *PORTION: ½ C, #8 dipper*

INGREDIENTS	10	20	30	40	50	60	70	80	90	100
Beets, canned, sliced	½ gal	1 gal	1½ gal	2 gal	2½ gal	3 gal	3½ gal	4 gal	4½ gal	5 gal
Brown Sugar	2 T	¼ C	⅓ C	½ C	½ C	¾ C	¾ C	1 C	1 C	1¼ C
Cornstarch	2 T	3 T	¼ C	⅓ C	½ C	½ C	¾ C	¾ C	1 C	1 C
Pineapple, crushed	1 lb 4 oz	2 lb 8 oz	3 lb 12 oz	5 lb	6 lb 4 oz	7 lb 8 oz	8 lb 12 oz	10 lb	11 lb 4 oz	12 lb 8 oz
Margarine, melted	1 oz	2 oz	3 oz	4 oz	5 oz	6 oz	7 oz	8 oz	9 oz	10 oz
Lemon Juice	2 T	¼ C	⅜ C	½ C	⅝ C	¾ C	⅞ C	1 C	1⅛ C	1¼ C

Nutrient Analysis per serving

Protein:	1 g
Carbohydrate:	25 g
Fat:	2 g
Sodium:	395 mg
Kilocalories:	122

Procedure

1. Drain beets. In a saucepan combine brown sugar, cornstarch, and undrained pineapple.
2. Cook and stir until thickened and bubbly.
3. Add margarine, lemon juice, and beets.
4. Cook and stir over medium heat until heated through.

GREEN BEANS AU GRATIN

CATEGORY: *Vegetable*   PORTION: ½ C, #8 dipper

INGREDIENTS	10	20	30	40	50	60	70	80	90	100
Green Beans, drained	3 lb	7 lb	10 lb	14 lb	17 lb	19 lb	24 lb	27 lb	31 lb	34 lb
Cream of Mushroom Soup, condensed	8 oz	1 lb	1 lb 8 oz	2 lb	2 lb 8 oz	3 lb 2 oz	3 lb 8 oz	4 lb	4 lb 8 oz	5 lb
American Cheese, grated	1 oz	2 oz	3 oz	4 oz	5 oz	6 oz	7 oz	8 oz	9 oz	10 oz

Nutrient Analysis per serving	Procedure

Nutrient Analysis per serving

Protein:	2 g
Carbohydrate:	7 g
Fat:	2 g
Sodium:	554 mg
Kilocalories:	59

Procedure

1. Mix ingredients lightly.
2. Place in shallow rectangular baking pan.
3. Sprinkle cheese over green beans.
4. Bake in a moderately hot oven 350°F for 30 minutes.

GREEN BEAN CASSEROLE

CATEGORY: *Vegetable*   PORTION: ½ C, #8 dipper

INGREDIENTS	10	20	30	40	50	60	70	80	90	100
Green Beans, canned	1 qt	2 qt	3 qt	5 qt	6 qt	7 qt	8 qt	9 qt	11 qt	12 qt
Cream of Mushroom Soup	8 oz	1 pt 2 oz	1 pt 12 oz	1 qt 6 oz	1 qt 16 oz	1 qt 24 oz	2 qt	2 qt 12 oz	2 qt 24 oz	3 qt
Fresh Onions, medium, thinly sliced	½	1	2	3	4	5	5	6	7	8

Nutrient Analysis per serving

Protein:	1 g
Carbohydrate:	5 g
Fat:	2 g
Sodium:	366 mg
Kilocalories:	42

Procedure

1. Mix together drained green beans and undiluted soup.
2. Pour into 2½" deep pans.
3. Slice onions thin and place on top.
4. Bake 30 minutes at 350°F.

SKILLET GREEN BEANS

CATEGORY: Vegetable   PORTION: ½ C, #8 dipper

INGREDIENTS	10	20	30	40	50	60	70	80	90	100
Bacon Slices, diced	2 oz	4 oz	8 oz	12 oz	1 lb	1 lb 2 oz	1 lb 4 oz	1 lb 8 oz	1 lb 12 oz	2 lb
Onions, chopped	2 oz	4 oz	8 oz	12 oz	1 lb	1 lb 2 oz	1 lb 4 oz	1 lb 8 oz	1 lb 12 oz	2 lb
Green Peppers, diced	1 T	2 T	3 T	4 T	5 T	6 T	7 T	8 T	9 T	10 T
Flour	1 T	1 oz	2 oz	3 oz	4 oz	5 oz	6 oz	7 oz	7 oz	8 oz
Green Beans, canned, drained (save the liquid)	1 qt 8 oz	2 qt 16 oz	3 qt	5 qt	6 qt	8 qt	9 qt	10 qt	11 qt	12 qt

Nutrient Analysis per serving

Protein:	4 g
Carbohydrate:	4 g
Fat:	5 g
Sodium:	352 mg
Kilocalories:	83

Procedure

1. Sauté bacon, onion, and green peppers, stirring until bacon is browned and vegetables are tender.
2. Reduce temperature.
3. Sprinkle flour over mixture, stir until smooth.
4. Add 3 cups of liquid from green beans and cook until slightly thickened.
5. Add green beans and simmer 10 minutes.

SUCCOTASH

INGREDIENTS	10	20	30	40	50	60	70	80	90	100
Lima Beans, frozen	1 lb 8 oz	3 lb	4 lb 8 oz	6 lb	7 lb 8 oz	9 lb	10 lb 8 oz	12 lb	13 lb 8 oz	15 lb
Water	¾ C	1½ C	2¼ C	3 C	3¾ C	4½ C	5¼ C	6 C	6¾ C	7½ C
Salt	½ t	1 t	1½ t	2 t	2½ t	3 t	3½ t	4 t	4½ t	5 t
Pepper	⅛ t	¼ t	⅜ t	½ t	⅝ t	¾ t	⅞ t	1 t	1⅛ t	1¼ t
Whole Kernel Corn, frozen	1 lb 8 oz	3 lb	4 lb 8 oz	6 lb	7 lb 8 oz	9 lb	10 lb 8 oz	12 lb	13 lb 8 oz	15 lb
Milk	1 C	2 C	3 C	1 qt	1 qt 8 oz	1 qt 16 oz	1 qt 24 oz	2 qt	2 qt 8 oz	2 qt 16 oz
Flour, all-purpose	2 oz	4 oz	6 oz	8 oz	10 oz	12 oz	14 oz	1 lb	1 lb 2 oz	1 lb 4 oz
Margarine	1 oz	2 oz	3 oz	4 oz	5 oz	6 oz	7 oz	8 oz	9 oz	10 oz

Nutrient Analysis per serving

Protein:	6 g
Carbohydrate:	30 g
Fat:	1 g
Sodium:	184 mg
Kilocalories:	155

Procedure

1. Cook lima beans, covered, in water, seasoned with salt and pepper for 10 minutes. Add frozen corn and return to boiling.
2. Reduce heat, cover, and cook 5 minutes more. Do not drain.
3. Gradually stir milk into flour. Stir flour mixture into vegetable mixture in saucepan.
4. Add margarine. Cook and stir until thickened and bubbly.

SWEET AND SOUR GREEN BEANS

CATEGORY: *Vegetable*   PORTION: *½ C, #8 dipper*

INGREDIENTS	10	20	30	40	50	60	70	80	90	100
Green Beans	1 qt	2 qt	3 qt	4 qt	5 qt	6 qt	7 qt	8 qt	9 qt	10 qt
Onions, medium, cut in rings	2	3	4	5	6	7	8	9	10	12
Bacon	8 oz	1 lb	1 lb 8 oz	2 lb	2 lb 8 oz	3 lb	3 lb 8 oz	4 lb	4 lb 8 oz	5 lb
Sugar	½ C	1 C	1½ C	2 C	2½ C	3 C	3½ C	4 C	4½ C	5 C
Vinegar	½ C	1 C	1½ C	2 C	2½ C	3 C	3½ C	4 C	4½ C	5 C

Nutrient Analysis per serving

Protein:	4 g
Carbohydrate:	12 g
Fat:	26 g
Sodium:	367 mg
Kilocalories:	301

Procedure

1. Drain beans and place in 4″ × 6″ deep steam-table pans.
2. Place separated onion rings over beans.
3. Fry bacon strips and save drippings. Cut strips in half and lay over onion rings.
4. Add sugar and vinegar to bacon drippings and heat.
5. Pour over the beans and marinate several hours or overnight.
6. Bake at 350°F for 45 minutes.

THREE-BEAN MEDLEY

CATEGORY: *Vegetable*   PORTION: ½ C, #8 dipper

INGREDIENTS	10	20	30	40	50	60	70	80	90	100
Green Beans, canned	1 pt 4 oz	1 qt 4 oz	1 qt 24 oz	2 qt 8 oz	3 qt	3 qt 20 oz	4 qt 4 oz	4 qt 24 oz	5 qt 8 oz	6 qt
Wax Beans, canned	1 pt 4 oz	1 qt 4 oz	1 qt 24 oz	2 qt 8 oz	3 qt	3 qt 20 oz	4 qt 4 oz	4 qt 24 oz	5 qt 8 oz	6 qt
Kidney Beans	8 oz	1 pt 4 oz	1 pt 12 oz	1 qt 6 oz	1 qt 16 oz	1 qt 26 oz	2 qt 4 oz	2 qt 12 oz	2 qt 20 oz	3 qt
Margarine, vegetable	1 oz	2 oz	3 oz	4 oz	5 oz	6 oz	7 oz	8 oz	9 oz	10 oz
Basil	½ t	1 t	1½ t	2 t	1 T	3½ t	4 t	4½ t	5 t	2 T
Marjoram	½ t	1 t	1½ t	2 t	1 T	3½ t	4 t	4½ t	5 t	2 T
Pepper, white	½ t	¾ t	1¼ t	1½ t	2 t	2½ t	2¾ t	3¼ t	3½ t	1½ T
Salt	¼ t	½ t	¾ t	1 t	1½ t	1¾ t	2 t	2¼ t	2½ t	1 T
Chicken Base	1 T	2 T	¼ C	⅓ C	½ C	½ C	⅔ C	⅔ C	¾ C	1 C
Oregano	¼ t	½ t	¾ t	1 t	1¼ t	1½ t	1¾ t	2 t	2¼ t	2½ t

Nutrient Analysis per serving

Protein:	2 g
Carbohydrate:	8 g
Fat:	2 g
Sodium:	253 mg
Kilocalories:	71

Procedure

1. Drain off half the liquid of each can of vegetables.
2. Combine vegetables and heat with remaining liquid in a stockpot.
3. Add seasonings and margarine.
4. Heat only long enough to bring to serving temperature (160°F to 170°F).
5. Transfer vegetables and liquid to steamtable pans.
6. Serve hot.

BAKED BROCCOLI

INGREDIENTS	10	20	30	40	50	60	70	80	90	100
Broccoli, frozen, cut	1 lb 8 oz	3 lb	4 lb 8 oz	6 lb 8 oz	8 lb	9 lb 8 oz	11 lb	12 lb 8 oz	14 lb 8 oz	16 lb
Salt	½ t	1 t	1½ t	1¾ t	2 t	2½ t	3 t	3½ t	3¾ t	4 t
Eggs, medium	2	3	5	6	8	9	10	12	14	16
Milk, 2%	½ C	1 C	1½ C	1¾ C	2 C	2½ C	3 C	3½ C	3¾ C	1 qt
Cheddar Cheese, grated	½ C	1 C	1½ C	1¾ C	2 C	2½ C	3 C	3½ C	3¾ C	1 qt
Pepper, black, ground	Pinch	⅛ t	¼ t	⅓ t	½ t	½ t	¾ t	¾ t	1 t	1 t

Nutrient Analysis per serving

Protein:	6 g
Carbohydrate:	4 g
Fat:	5 g
Sodium:	218 mg
Kilocalories:	87

Procedure

1. Cook broccoli until barely tender. Drain well and sprinkle with salt.
2. Beat eggs and add milk, cheese, and pepper.
3. Add broccoli and mix. Pour into greased baking pan.
4. Place pan in pan with 1″ water and bake at 350°F for 1 hour until browned. *Do Not Overcook.*

HOLIDAY BROCCOLI CASSEROLE

CATEGORY: Vegetable   *PORTION: ½ C, #8 dipper*

INGREDIENTS	10	20	30	40	50	60	70	80	90	100
Broccoli, chopped, frozen	2 lb	3 lb	4 lb	6 lb	8 lb	10 lb	11 lb	12 lb	14 lb	16 lb
Margarine, melted	1 oz	2 oz	4 oz	6 oz	8 oz	10 oz	12 oz	14 oz	1 lb	1 lb 2 oz
Flour, all-purpose	1 T	1 oz	1½ oz	2 oz	3 oz	3½ oz	4 oz	4½ oz	5 oz	6 oz
Chicken Soup Base	2 t	1 T	2 T	3 T	4 T	4½ T	5 T	6 T	7 T	8 T
Salt	¼ t	½ t	¾ t	1 t	1½ t	1¾ t	2 t	2¾ t	3 t	1 T
Milk, 2%	1 C	2 C	4 C	5 C	6 C	7 C	8 C	10 C	11 C	12 C
Margarine, 2nd	1 oz	2 oz	4 oz	5 oz	6 oz	7 oz	8 oz	10 oz	11 oz	12 oz
Water, hot 180°F	½ C	¾ C	1¼ C	1½ C	2 C	2½ C	2¾ C	3 C	3½ C	4 C
Stuffing Mix, herb seasoned	4 oz	8 oz	1 lb	1 lb 2 oz	1 lb 8 oz	1 lb 12 oz	1 lb 8 oz	1 lb 12 oz	2 lb	3 lb

Nutrient Analysis per serving

Protein:	5 g
Carbohydrate:	10 g
Fat:	7 g
Sodium:	431 mg
Kilocalories:	122

Procedure

1. Thaw broccoli and place in perforated pans. Steam for 10 to 15 minutes. Drain well.
2. Blend melted margarine, flour, chicken stock base, and salt. Heat over low flame. *Do Not Brown.* Add milk. Cook and stir until thickened.
3. Melt 2nd margarine in hot water and pour over stuffing mix.
4. Place broccoli into greased pans. Pour white sauce into each pan and top with bread crumb mixture.
5. Bake in 400°F oven for 25 to 30 minutes.

COMPANY CABBAGE

INGREDIENTS	10	20	30	40	50	60	70	80	90	100
Beef Bouillon Granules, instant	1 t	2 t	1 T	1½ T	1½ T	2 T	2½ T	2½ T	3 T	3 T
Cabbage, coarsely shredded	1 lb 8 oz	3 lb	4 lb 8 oz	6 lb	7 lb 8 oz	9 lb	10 lb 8 oz	12 lb	13 lb 8 oz	15 lb
Carrots, coarsely shredded	8 oz	1 lb	1 lb 8 oz	2 lb	2 lb 8 oz	3 lb	3 lb 8 oz	4 lb	4 lb 8 oz	5 lb
Onion, chopped	½ C	1 C	1½ C	2 C	2½ C	3 C	3½ C	4 C	4½ C	5 C
Margarine, melted	1 oz	2 oz	3 oz	4 oz	5 oz	6 oz	7 oz	8 oz	9 oz	10 oz
Mustard, prepared	2 T	¼ C	⅓ C	½ C	½ C	¾ C	¾ C	1 C	1 C	1¼ C
Pepper	¼ t	½ t	¾ t	1 t	1¼ t	1½ t	1¾ t	2 t	2¼ t	2½ t

Nutrient Analysis per serving

Protein:	1 g
Carbohydrate:	7 g
Fat:	2 g
Sodium:	178 mg
Kilocalories:	57

Procedure

1. In small amount of water, heat bouillon granules until dissolved. Add cabbage, carrots, onions, and pepper. Toss to mix.
2. Cook, covered, over medium heat until tender, stirring once during cooking. Drain if necessary.
3. Combine butter and mustard. Pour over vegetables; toss to mix. Spoon into pan or dish.

SCALLOPED CABBAGE

INGREDIENTS	10	20	30	40	50	60	70	80	90	100
Cabbage, medium heads	1½	3	4½	6	8	9½	11	12½	14	16
Margarine	1 oz	2 oz	3 oz	4 oz	5 oz	6 oz	7 oz	8 oz	9 oz	10 oz
Flour	2 T	¼ C	⅓ C	½ C	¾ C	¾ C	1 C	1¼ C	1⅓ C	1½ C
Milk	6 oz	12 oz	1 pt 2 oz	1 pt 8 oz	1 qt	1 qt 6 oz	1 qt 12 oz	1 qt 16 oz	1 qt 24 oz	2 qt
Evaporated Milk	6 oz	12 oz	1 pt 2 oz	1 pt 8 oz	1 qt	1 qt 6 oz	1 qt 12 oz	1 qt 16 oz	1 qt 24 oz	2 qt
American Cheese, shredded	6 oz	12 oz	1 lb 2 oz	1 lb 8 oz	2 lb	2 lb 6 oz	2 lb 12 oz	2 lb 16 oz	2 lb 24 oz	4 lb
Salt and Pepper, to taste										
Buttered Bread Crumbs	½ C	1 C	1½ C	2 C	2½ C	3 C	3½ C	4 C	4½ C	5 C

Nutrient Analysis per serving

Protein:	7 g
Carbohydrate:	10 g
Fat:	10 g
Sodium:	360 mg
Kilocalories:	159

Procedure

1. Quarter cabbage and simmer in small amounts of water for 8 minutes and drain.
2. Melt margarine and mix in flour. Add milk and evaporated milk. Mix until sauce is smooth. Heat to boiling, stirring constantly.
3. Remove from heat and add cheese, salt, and pepper.
4. Place cabbage in baking dish, top with sauce, then with crumbs.
5. Bake in 300°F oven for 30 minutes or until crumbs brown.

BAKED FRESH CARROTS

CATEGORY: *Vegetable*   PORTION: *4 oz*

INGREDIENTS	10	20	30	40	50	60	70	80	90	100
Carrots, peeled and cut lengthwise	2 lb	4 lb	6 lb	8 lb	10 lb	12 lb	14 lb	16 lb	18 lb	20 lb
Brown Sugar	4 oz	8 oz	12 oz	1 lb	1 lb 4 oz	1 lb 8 oz	1 lb 12 oz	2 lb	2 lb 4 oz	2 lb 8 oz
Margarine	3 oz	6 oz	9 oz	12 oz	1 lb 3 oz	1 lb 6 oz	1 lb 9 oz	1 lb 12 oz	2 lb	2 lb 6 oz

Nutrient Analysis per serving

Protein:	1 g
Carbohydrate:	20 g
Fat:	2 g
Sodium:	142 mg
Kilocalories:	142

Procedure

1. Cook carrots until tender; drain.
2. Place in greased baking pan.
3. Heat sugar in margarine; pour over carrots.
4. Bake in 375°F oven for 25 minutes.

GLAZED CARROTS

INGREDIENTS	10	20	30	40	50	60	70	80	90	100
Carrots, frozen	2 lb 8 oz	5 lb	7 lb	10 lb	12 lb	14 lb 8 oz	17 lb	19 lb	22 lb	24 lb
Margarine	2 oz	4 oz	6 oz	8 oz	12 oz	14 oz	1 lb	1 lb 2 oz	1 lb 4 oz	1 lb 8 oz
Sugar	1 oz	2 oz	4 oz	6 oz	8 oz	10 oz	12 oz	1 lb	1 lb 2 oz	1 lb 4 oz
Salt	¾ t	1½ t	2½ t	1 T	1½ T	1¾ T	2 T	2½ T	2¾ T	3 T

Nutrient Analysis per serving

Protein:	1 g
Carbohydrate:	14 g
Fat:	4 g
Sodium:	293 mg
Kilocalories:	101

Procedure

1. Cook carrots and drain.
2. Melt margarine, sugar, and salt.
3. Pour over carrots.
4. Bake at 400°F for 15 to 20 minutes.

LYONNAISE CARROTS

INGREDIENTS	10	20	30	40	50	60	70	80	90	100
Carrots, sliced	3 lb	6 lb	8 lb	11 lb	14 lb	17 lb	20 lb	22 lb	25 lb	28 lb
Onions, sliced	3 lb	6 lb	8 lb	11 lb	14 lb	17 lb	20 lb	22 lb	25 lb	28 lb
Salt	1 t	2 t	1 T	1½ T	2 T	2½ T	3 T	3½ T	4 T	4½ T
Margarine	2 oz	3 oz	4 oz	6 oz	8 oz	10 oz	11 oz	12 oz	14 oz	1 lb
Pepper	Dash	⅛ t	¼ t	½ t	¾ t	1 t	1⅛ t	1¼ t	1½ t	1¾ t
Beef Stock	1 pt 2 oz	1 qt 6 oz	1 qt 24 oz	2 qt 12 oz	3 qt	3 qt 16 oz	1 gal	5 qt	5 qt 16 oz	6 qt

Nutrient Analysis per serving

Protein: 1 g
Carbohydrate: 13 g
Fat: 3 g
Sodium: 218 mg
Kilocalories: 90

Procedure

1. Alternate layers of carrots and onions in baking pan, sprinkling each layer with salt, small pieces of margarine, and pepper to taste.
2. Add beef stock and place in a moderate oven for 90 minutes, allowing to simmer until most of the stock is absorbed by the vegetables.

CAULIFLOWER AU GRATIN

CATEGORY: *Vegetable*   PORTION: *#8 scoop*

INGREDIENTS	10	20	30	40	50	60	70	80	90	100
Cauliflower, frozen	2 lb 8 oz	5 lb	7 lb 8 oz	10 lb	12 lb 8 oz	15 lb	17 lb 8 oz	20 lb	22 lb 8 oz	25 lb
Light Cheese Sauce	1 pt 8 oz	1 qt 16 oz	2 qt 8 oz	3 qt	3 qt 24 oz	1 gal 16 oz	1 gal 40 oz	1 gal 2 qt	1 gal 3 qt	2 gal
Bread Crumbs	½ C	1 C	1½ C	2 C	2½ C	3 C	3½ C	4 C	4½ C	5 C
Paprika	½ t	1 t	1½ t	2 t	2½ t	3 t	3½ t	4 t	4½ t	5 t
Butter or Margarine, melted	1 T	2 T	3 T	4 T	5 T	6 T	7 T	8 T	9 T	10 T

Nutrient Analysis per serving

Protein:	8 g
Carbohydrate:	9 g
Fat:	12 g
Sodium:	340 mg
Kilocalories:	175

Procedure

1. Place cauliflower in rapidly boiling water (salted). When water returns to a boil, reduce heat and cook until just tender. Drain. Do not overcook.
2. Place drained cauliflower in lightly greased baking pan and cover with cheese sauce.
3. Combine bread crumbs and paprika and sprinkle over sauce. Drizzle with melted butter.
4. Bake in 350°F oven for 20 minutes or until nicely browned and bubbly. Serve with #8 dipper.

CORN FRITTERS

INGREDIENTS	10	20	30	40	50	60	70	80	90	100
Eggs, medium	3	5	8	10	12	15	17	20	22	24
Sugar, granulated	2 oz	3 oz	4 oz	5 oz	6 oz	7 oz	8 oz	9 oz	10 oz	12 oz
Oil, vegetable	1 T	2 T	3 T	4 T	5 T	6 T	7 T	8 T	9 T	10 T
Milk, whole	6 oz	12 oz	1 pt 4 oz	1 pt 8 oz	1 qt	1 qt 4 oz	1 qt 8 oz	1 qt 16 oz	1 qt 24 oz	2 qt
Nutmeg	½ t	1 t	1½ t	2 t	2½ t	1 T	3½ t	4 t	4½ t	5 t
Corn, canned, whole kernel, drained	1 C	2 C	3 C	4 C	4½ C	5½ C	6½ C	7½ C	8½ C	9 C
Flour, all-purpose	12 oz	1 lb 8 oz	2 lb 6 oz	3 lb	3 lb 12 oz	4 lb 8 oz	5 lb 4 oz	6 lb 2 oz	6 lb 12 oz	7 lb 8 oz
Baking Powder	1 T	2 T	3 T	4 T	5 T	6 T	7 T	8 T	9 T	10 T
Salt	1½ t	1 T	1½ T	2 T	2½ T	3 T	3½ T	4 T	4½ T	5 T

Nutrient Analysis per serving

Protein:	6 g
Carbohydrate:	35 g
Fat:	8 g
Sodium:	494 mg
Kilocalories:	245

Procedure

1. Beat eggs with sugar. Add oil, milk, and nutmeg until well blended.
2. Drain corn; place in bowl with eggs.
3. Combine flour, baking powder, and salt; add to egg mixture.
4. Stir lightly until ingredients are blended. Do not overmix.
5. Heat frying fat to 360°F. Drop batter into fat with #24 scoop; fry until brown and cooked through, about 7 minutes. Do not cover while keeping hot.
6. Serve 2 fritters with sausage and syrup.

CORN PUDDING

INGREDIENTS	10	20	30	40	50	60	70	80	90	100
Corn, canned, cream-style	1 qt 16 oz	3 qt	4 qt	5 qt	6 qt	8 qt	9 qt	10 qt	11 qt	12 qt
Sugar	1 T	2 T	3 T	4 T	5 T	6 T	7 T	8 T	9 T	10 T
Salt	1 t	1½ t	2 t	2½ t	3 t	3½ t	4 t	4½ t	5 t	5 t
Milk	6 oz	12 oz	1 pt 2 oz	1 qt 1 pt	2 qt	2 qt 6 oz	3 qt 6 oz	3 qt 2 oz	3 qt 2 oz	4 qt
Eggs, beaten	2	5	7	10	12	14	17	19	22	24
Bread Crumbs	6 oz	12 oz	1 lb	1 lb 8 oz	2 lb	2 lb 6 oz	2 lb 12 oz	3 lb	3 lb 8 oz	4 lb

Nutrient Analysis per serving

Protein:	42 g
Carbohydrate:	6 g
Fat:	2 g
Sodium:	806 mg
Kilocalories:	208

Procedure

1. Combine all ingredients; heat to just below boiling, stirring constantly over low heat.
2. Pour corn mixture into a buttered baking pan; bake about 1 hour or until center is set. The pan may be placed in a pan of hot water to reduce danger of curdling.

CORN O'BRIEN

CATEGORY: Vegetable   PORTION: ½ C, #8 dipper

INGREDIENTS	10	20	30	40	50	60	70	80	90	100
Corn, canned	1 qt	2 qt	4 qt	5 qt	6 qt	7 qt	9 qt	10 qt	11 qt	12 qt
Green Pepper, chopped	4 oz	8 oz	10 oz	12 oz	1 lb	1 lb 4 oz	1 lb 8 oz	1 lb 10 oz	1 lb 12 oz	2 lb
Onions, dehydrated	4 oz	8 oz	10 oz	12 oz	1 lb	1 lb 4 oz	1 lb 8 oz	1 lb 10 oz	1 lb 12 oz	2 lb
Salt	½ t	1 t	1½ t	1 T	3½ t	4 t	4½ t	5 t	5½ t	2 T
Pepper, white	¼ t	½ t	¾ t	1 t	1¼ t	1½ t	1¾ t	2 t	2¼ t	2½ t
Bacon	4 oz	8 oz	12 oz	1 lb	1 lb 4 oz	1 lb 8 oz	1 lb 12 oz	2 lb	2 lb 4 oz	2 lb 8 oz
Pimientos	2 oz	4 oz	5 oz	6 oz	8 oz	10 oz	12 oz	14 oz	1 lb	1 lb 2 oz

Nutrient Analysis per serving

Protein: 3 g
Carbohydrate: 22 g
Fat: 7 g
Sodium: 346 mg
Kilocalories: 155

Procedure

1. Drain corn.
2. Sauté chopped bacon, green peppers, onion, salt, and white pepper.
3. Add to drained corn.
4. Cook until heated thoroughly.
5. Add pimientos prior to serving.

CORN PUDDING WITH CHEESE

CATEGORY: *Vegetable*   PORTION: *#8 scoop*

INGREDIENTS	10	20	30	40	50	60	70	80	90	100
Mustard, powdered	1 t	2 t	1 T	4 t	5 t	2 T	7 t	8 t	3 T	10 t
Water	1 t	2 t	1 T	4 t	5 t	2 T	7 t	8 t	3 T	10 t
Butter or Margarine	3 oz	6 oz	8 oz	12 oz	1 lb	1 lb 4 oz	1 lb 8 oz	1 lb 10 oz	1 lb 12 oz	2 lb
Flour	2 oz	4 oz	6 oz	8 oz	10 oz	12 oz	14 oz	1 lb	1 lb 2 oz	1 lb 4 oz
Milk	1 pt 4 oz	1 qt 8 oz	2 qt	2 qt 16 oz	3 qt 4 oz	3 qt 24 oz	1 gal 12 oz	1 gal 1 qt	1 gal 3 pt	1 gal 2 qt
Cheddar Cheese, shredded	8 oz	1 lb 4 oz	1 lb 14 oz	2 lb 8 oz	3 lb 2 oz	3 lb 12 oz	4 lb 6 oz	5 lb	5 lb 10 oz	6 lb 4 oz
Corn, drained	2½ C	1 qt 8 oz	2 qt	2 qt 16 oz	3 qt 4 oz	3 qt 24 oz	1 gal 12 oz	1 gal 1 qt	1 gal 3 pt	1 gal 2 qt
Bread Crumbs, soft	1 pt	1 qt	3 pt	2 qt	5 pt	3 qt	3 qt 1 pt	1 gal	1 gal 1 pt	1 gal 1 qt
Salt	½ T	1 T	1½ T	2 T	2½ T	3 T	3½ T	4 T	4½ T	5 T
Sugar	1 t	2 t	1 T	4 t	5 t	2 T	7 t	8 t	3 T	10 t
Pepper	½ t	1 t	1½ t	2 t	2⅓ t	3 t	3½ t	4 t	5 t	6 t
Eggs, beaten	7	14	21	28	35	40	47	54	61	68

Nutrient Analysis per serving

Protein:	14.8 g
Carbohydrate:	17.5 g
Fat:	21.0 g
Sodium:	557 mg
Kilocalories:	314

Procedure

1. Combine mustard and water; let stand 10 minutes for flavor to develop.
2. Melt butter; blend in flour.
3. Gradually stir in milk; cook and stir over low heat until thickened and smooth.
4. Remove from heat. Add mustard and remaining ingredients; mix well.
5. Turn into greased baking pan or pans. Place in pan of hot water. Bake in 325°F oven 1 hour 15 minutes or until knife inserted in center comes out clean.

PEAS AND MUSHROOMS

CATEGORY: *Vegetable*   PORTION: *4 oz*

INGREDIENTS	10	20	30	40	50	60	70	80	90	100
Frozen Peas	10 oz	1 lb 4 oz	1 lb 14 oz	2 lb 8 oz	3 lb 2 oz	3 lb 12 oz	4 lb 6 oz	5 lb	5 lb 10 oz	6 lb 4 oz
Fresh Mushrooms, sliced	1 lb	2 lb	3 lb	4 lb	5 lb	6 lb	7 lb	8 lb	9 lb	10 lb
Onion, fresh, chopped	4 oz	8 oz	12 oz	1 lb	1 lb 4 oz	1 lb 8 oz	1 lb 12 oz	2 lb	2 lb 4 oz	2 lb 8 oz
Margarine	1 oz	2 oz	3 oz	4 oz	5 oz	6 oz	7 oz	8 oz	9 oz	10 oz
Sugar	1 T	2 T	3 T	¼ C	⅓ C	½ C	½ C	½ C	½ C	¾ C
Salt	½ t	1 t	1½ t	2 t	2½ t	3 t	3½ t	4 t	4½ t	5 t

Nutrient Analysis per serving

Protein:	2 g
Carbohydrate:	7 g
Fat:	2 g
Sodium:	175 mg
Kilocalories:	64

Procedure

1. Cook peas according to package directions. Drain well.
2. Cook mushrooms and onion in margarine until tender.
3. Stir in sugar and salt. Add cooked peas. Cover and heat through.

CHEESE POTATOES

INGREDIENTS	10	20	30	40	50	60	70	80	90	100
Potato Wedges, boiled and drained	4 lb	8 lb	12 lb	16 lb	20 lb	24 lb	28 lb	32 lb	36 lb	40 lb
Margarine	2 T	¼ C	⅓ C	½ C	⅔ C	¾ C	¾ C	1 C	1¼ C	1⅓ C
American Cheese, grated	8 oz	1 lb	1 lb 8 oz	2 lb	2 lb 8 oz	3 lb	3 lb 8 oz	4 lb	4 lb 8 oz	5 lb

Nutrient Analysis per serving

Protein:	8 g
Carbohydrate:	34 g
Fat:	8 g
Sodium:	308 mg
Kilocalories:	236

Procedure

1. Place potatoes in greased rectangular baking pan.
2. Chop margarine and scatter over potatoes.
3. Sprinkle cheese over potatoes.
4. Bake at 325°F for 20 to 30 minutes until cheese melts.

DUCHESS POTATOES

CATEGORY: *Vegetable*   PORTION: ½ C, #8 dipper

INGREDIENTS	10	20	30	40	50	60	70	80	90	100
Potatoes, pared	3 lb	6 lb	9 lb	12 lb	15 lb	18 lb	21 lb	24 lb	27 lb	30 lb
Milk, hot	1 pt	1 pt 8 oz	1 qt 6 oz	1 qt 16 oz	2 qt	2 qt 12 oz	2 pt 24 oz	3 qt 6 oz	3 qt 16 oz	4 qt
Margarine	2 oz	3 oz	4 oz	6 oz	8 oz	10 oz	11 oz	12 oz	14 oz	1 lb
Salt	2 t	1 T	2 T	3 T	4 T	5 T	6 T	7 T	8 T	10 T
Eggs	4	7	11	14	18	22	25	29	32	36

Nutrient Analysis per serving

Protein:	6 g
Carbohydrate:	26 g
Fat:	7 g
Sodium:	551 mg
Kilocalories:	197

Procedure

1. Peel and eye potatoes and cut into uniform size pieces. Steam or boil. When done, drain, and place in mixer bowl.
2. Mash until there are no lumps.
3. Add beaten eggs to the mashed potatoes.
4. Pile lightly into baking pans. Bake at 350°F for 20 to 30 minutes, or until set.

MUSHROOM POTATOES

CATEGORY: *Vegetable*   PORTION: ½ C, #8 dipper

INGREDIENTS	10	20	30	40	50	60	70	80	90	100
Cream of Mushroom Soup	1 pt	1 qt	1 qt 16 oz	2 qt	2 qt 16 oz	3 qt	3 qt 16 oz	4 qt	4 qt 16 oz	5 qt
Potatoes, dehydrated, sliced, (or diced fresh)	8 oz	1 lb	1 lb 8 oz	2 lb	2 lb 8 oz	3 lb	3 lb 8 oz	4 lb	4 lb 8 oz	5 lb
Milk, 2%	8 oz	1 pt	1 pt 8 oz	1 qt	1 qt 8 oz	1 qt 16 oz	1 qt 24 oz	2 qt	2 qt 8 oz	2 qt 16 oz

Nutrient Analysis per serving

Protein:	3 g
Carbohydrate:	18 g
Fat:	5 g
Sodium:	383 mg
Kilocalories:	138

Procedure

1. Soak dehydrated potatoes in water overnight or for 8 hours.
2. Drain and place in baking pans.
3. Mix soup and milk together. Heat and pour over potatoes.
4. Bake at 350°F for 1 hour.

OVEN BROWNED POTATOES

CATEGORY: *Vegetable*   PORTION: ½ C, #8 dipper

INGREDIENTS	10	20	30	40	50	60	70	80	90	100
Potatoes	10	20	30	40	50	60	70	80	90	100
Margarine, melted	4 oz	8 oz	10 oz	12 oz	1 lb	1 lb 4 oz	1 lb 8 oz	1 lb 10 oz	1 lb 12 oz	2 lb

Nutrient Analysis per serving

Protein:	2 g
Carbohydrate:	16 g
Fat:	9 g
Sodium:	128 mg
Kilocalories:	152

Procedure

1. Peel potatoes.
2. Parboil for 10 minutes in salted water. Drain off water.
3. Place potatoes in shallow greased baking pan.
4. Pour melted margarine over potatoes.
5. Bake at 350°F, turning often until potatoes are golden brown (about 1 hour).

PEPPY POTATOES

INGREDIENTS	10	20	30	40	50	60	70	80	90	100
Potatoes	4 lb	8 lb	12 lb	16 lb	20 lb	24 lb	28 lb	32 lb	36 lb	40 lb
Margarine, melted	¼ C	⅓ C	½ C	¾ C	1 C	1¼ C	1⅓ C	1½ C	1¾ C	2 C
Corn Flake Crumbs	1 C	2 C	3 C	4 C	5 C	6 C	7 C	8 C	9 C	10 C

Nutrient Analysis per serving

Protein:	3 g
Carbohydrate:	33 g
Fat:	4 g
Sodium:	102 mg
Kilocalories:	184

Procedure

1. Scrub potatoes and cut, unpeeled, into 1″ wedge.
2. Roll potato pieces a few at a time in melted margarine to coat.
3. Roll margarined potatoes in crumbs and place in single layer on greased cookie sheet.
4. Bake in 350°F oven for 50 minutes.

POTATO CHEESE PUFF

CATEGORY: *Vegetable*   PORTION: ½ C, #8 dipper

INGREDIENTS	10	20	30	40	50	60	70	80	90	100
Mashed Potatoes, instant	6 oz	12 oz	1 lb 4 oz	1 lb 8 oz	2 lb	2 lb 6 oz	2 lb 12 oz	3 lb 4 oz	3 lb 8 oz	4 lb
Onion, fresh, medium, chopped	2 oz	4 oz	6 oz	8 oz	10 oz	12 oz	1 lb	1 lb 2 oz	1 lb 4 oz	1 lb 8 oz
Eggs, medium	5	10	14	19	24	29	34	38	43	48
Milk, whole	6 oz	12 oz	1 pt 2 oz	1 pt 8 oz	1 qt	1 qt 6 oz	1 qt 12 oz	1 qt 16 oz	1 qt 24 oz	2 qt
American Cheese, diced	6 oz	12 oz	1 lb 4 oz	1 lb 8 oz	2 lb	2 lb 5 oz	2 lb 12 oz	3 lb 4 oz	3 lb 8 oz	4 lb

Nutrient Analysis per serving

Protein:	7 g
Carbohydrate:	5 g
Fat:	8 g
Sodium:	300 mg
Kilocalories:	126

Procedure

1. Prepare instant potatoes according to package directions for number of servings listed.
2. Beat egg with a wire whisk until fluffy.
3. Mix together chopped onion, eggs, milk, mashed potatoes, and diced cheese.
4. Pour into a greased baking pan.
5. Bake at 375°F for 50 minutes or until a knife inserted in the center comes out clean.

POTATOES O'BRIEN

CATEGORY: *Vegetable*   PORTION: ½ C, #8 dipper

INGREDIENTS	10	20	30	40	50	60	70	80	90	100
Bacon	8 oz	1 lb	1 lb 8 oz	2 lb	2 lb 8 oz	3 lb	3 lb 8 oz	4 lb	4 lb 8 oz	5 lb
Onions, diced	2 T	¼ C	⅓ C	½ C	½ C	⅔ C	¾ C	1 C	1¼ C	1½ C
Green Peppers, diced	2 T	¼ C	⅓ C	½ C	½ C	⅔ C	¾ C	1 C	1¼ C	1½ C
Margarine, melted	2 oz	4 oz	6 oz	8 oz	10 oz	12 oz	14 oz	1 lb	1 lb 2 oz	1 lb 4 oz
Pimientos, finely diced	2 oz	4 oz	6 oz	8 oz	10 oz	12 oz	14 oz	1 lb	1 lb 2 oz	1 lb 4 oz
Cider Vinegar	2 T	¼ C	⅓ C	½ C	½ C	⅔ C	¾ C	1 C	1¼ C	1½ C
Potatoes, whole, frozen	2 lb	4 lb	6 lb	10 lb	11 lb	13 lb	15 lb	20 lb	21 lb	22 lb

Nutrient Analysis per serving

Protein:	4 g
Carbohydrate:	16 g
Fat:	17 g
Sodium:	230 mg
Kilocalories:	240

Procedure

1. Fry bacon until done, but not crisp.
2. Remove bacon and chop. Set aside.
3. Discard half the bacon grease.
4. Sauté onions and green peppers in margarine and bacon grease.
5. Add pimientos, cooked bacon, and vinegar to sautéed vegetables and keep warm.
6. Place frozen potatoes into greased baking pans and bake at 350°F for 45 minutes.
7. Add warm bacon mixture to cooked potatoes.

SCALLOPED POTATOES

CATEGORY: *Vegetable*   PORTION: *#8 scoop*

INGREDIENTS	10	20	30	40	50	60	70	80	90	100
Margarine or Butter	4 oz	6 oz	8 oz	12 oz	1 lb	1 lb 4 oz	1 lb 6 oz	1 lb 8 oz	1 lb 12 oz	2 lb
Potatoes, peeled and sliced	2 lb 6 oz	4 lb 12 oz	7 lb 2 oz	9 lb 8 oz	12 lb	14 lb 6 oz	16 lb 12 oz	19 lb 2 oz	21 lb 8 oz	24 lb
Salt	¼ t	½ t	¾ t	1 t	1¼ t	1½ t	1¾ t	2 t	2¼ t	2½ t
Pepper	¼ t	½ t	¾ t	1 t	1¼ t	1½ t	1¾ t	2 t	2¼ t	2½ t
Milk, scalded	1 pt 8 oz	1 qt 16 oz	2 qt 8 oz	3 qt	3 qt 24 oz	1 gal 16 oz	1 gal 1 qt	1 gal 2 qt	1 gal 3 qt	2 gal

Nutrient Analysis per serving

Protein:	6 g
Carbohydrate:	21 g
Fat:	8 g
Sodium:	722 mg
Kilocalories:	192

Procedure

1. Grease baking pans. Place a layer of potatoes in the bottom and season with salt and pepper. Dot with margarine.
2. Continue layers until all potatoes are used.
3. Pour on milk until even with top layer of potatoes.
4. Cover and bake 350°F for 30 minutes.
5. Remove cover and continue cooking until potatoes are tender when pierced with a fork.

SCALLOPED POTATOES WITH CHEESE

CATEGORY: *Vegetable*   PORTION: *#8 scoop*

INGREDIENTS	10	20	30	40	50	60	70	80	90	100
Potatoes, raw, white, sliced	2 lb 8 oz	5 lb	7 lb 8 oz	10 lb	12 lb 8 oz	15 lb	17 lb 8 oz	20 lb	22 lb 8 oz	25 lb
Cream of Chicken Soup, condensed	1 pt 4 oz	1 qt 8 oz	2 qt	2 qt 16 oz	3 qt	3 qt 24 oz	1 gal 12 oz	1 gal 1 qt	1 gal 3 pt	1 gal 2 qt
Milk	½ C	1 C	1½ C	2 C	2½ C	3 C	3½ C	4 C	4½ C	5 C
American Cheese, shredded	4 oz	10 oz	1 lb	1 lb 4 oz	1 lb 8 oz	2 lb	2 lb 4 oz	2 lb 10 oz	3 lb	3 lb 4 oz
Bread Crumbs, buttered	½ C	1 C	1½ C	2 C	2½ C	3 C	3½ C	4 C	4½ C	5 C

Nutrient Analysis per serving

Protein:	6 g
Carbohydrate:	21 g
Fat:	8 g
Sodium:	722 mg
Kilocalories:	192

Procedure

1. Boil or steam potatoes; drain if necessary.
2. Combine soup and milk; heat to simmer. Add cheese, stirring until melted. Add more milk if necessary.
3. Combine sauce and potatoes. Turn into a baking dish and sprinkle with buttered crumbs.
4. Bake in 400°F oven 45 minutes or until mixture is thoroughly hot and surface is golden.

AU GRATIN SPINACH

INGREDIENTS	10	20	30	40	50	60	70	80	90	100
Margarine	2 oz	3 oz	4 oz	5 oz	8 oz	10 oz	11 oz	12 oz	13 oz	1 lb
Flour	2 oz	3 oz	4 oz	5 oz	8 oz	10 oz	11 oz	12 oz	13 oz	1 lb
Mustard, dry	¼ t	½ t	1¼ t	1½ t	2 t	2¼ t	2½ t	3¼ t	3½ t	4 t
Salt	¼ t	½ t	1¼ t	1½ t	2 t	2¼ t	2½ t	3¼ t	3½ t	4 t
Pepper	Pinch	Pinch	⅛ t	⅛ t	¼ t	¼ t	¼ t	½ t	½ t	½ t
Bread Crumbs	2 oz	6 oz	8 oz	12 oz	1 lb	1 lb 3 oz	1 lb 6 oz	1 lb 8 oz	1 lb 12 oz	2 lb
Milk, 2%, scalded	12 oz	24 oz	1 qt 4 oz	1 qt 16 oz	2 qt	2 qt 12 oz	2 qt 24 oz	3 qt 4 oz	3 qt 16 oz	4 qt
Spinach, frozen, drained	2 lb 8 oz	5 lb	7 lb 8 oz	10 lb	12 lb 8 oz	15 lb	17 lb 8 oz	20 lb	22 lb 8 oz	25 lb
Cheese, grated	6 oz	12 oz	1 lb 2 oz	1 lb 8 oz	2 lb	2 lb 6 oz	2 lb 12 oz	3 lb 2 oz	3 lb 8 oz	4 lb

Nutrient Analysis per serving

Protein:	9 g
Carbohydrate:	15 g
Fat:	10 g
Sodium:	427 mg
Kilocalories:	189

Procedure

1. Combine melted margarine, flour, mustard, salt, and pepper.
2. Add milk gradually and stir until thickened.
3. Add drained spinach and about ⅔ of the cheese to the sauce. Stir until the cheese is melted.
4. Put into rectangular baking pan.
5. Mix remaining cheese with crumbs and sprinkle over spinach. Bake at 400°F for 30 minutes.

COUNTRY SPINACH

CATEGORY: *Vegetable*   PORTION: ½ C, #8 dipper

INGREDIENTS	10	20	30	40	50	60	70	80	90	100
Spinach, frozen, chopped	1 lb 8 oz	3 lb	4 lb 8 oz	6 lb	8 lb	9 lb 8 oz	11 lb	12 lb 8 oz	14 lb	16 lb
Bacon, sliced	6 oz	12 oz	1 lb 2 oz	1 lb 8 oz	1 lb 12 oz	2 lb 4 oz	2 lb 8 oz	2 lb 12 oz	3 lb	3 lb 4 oz
Flour	2 oz	4 oz	6 oz	8 oz	8 oz	10 oz	10 oz	12 oz	14 oz	1 lb
Evaporated milk	1 C	2 C	3 C	1 qt	1 qt 8 oz	1 qt 16 oz	1 qt 24 oz	2 qt	2 qt 8 oz	2 qt 16 oz
Salt	1 t	2 t	1 T	1 T	2 T	2 T	2½ T	2½ T	3 T	3 T
Onion, fresh, grated	1 oz	2 oz	2 oz	4 oz	4 oz	6 oz	6 oz	8 oz	8 oz	10 oz
Vinegar	1 t	2 t	1 T	1 T	2 T	2 T	3 T	3 T	4 T	4 T

Nutrient Analysis per serving

Protein:	5 g
Carbohydrate:	9 g
Fat:	10 g
Sodium:	400 mg
Kilocalories:	156

Procedure

1. Cook spinach until tender and drain well, reserving liquid.
2. Fry bacon until crisp; stir in flour.
3. Add milk, salt, and onion; mix in liquid from cooked spinach.
4. Cook over low heat until thickened.
5. Crumble bacon into sauce; stir in vinegar.
6. Pour over spinach and mix lightly.

SPINACH SOUFFLÉ

CATEGORY: Vegetable   *PORTION: #8 dipper*

INGREDIENTS	10	20	30	40	50	60	70	80	90	100
Margarine	4 oz	8 oz	12 oz	1 lb	1 lb 4 oz	1 lb 8 oz	1 lb 12 oz	2 lb	2 lb 4 oz	2 lb 8 oz
Flour	1½ T	3 T	2 oz	3 oz	4 oz	5 oz	6 oz	7 oz	8 oz	9 oz
Salt	Dash	Dash	⅛ t	¼ t	½ t	½ t	¾ t	¾ t	1 t	1 t
Milk	8 oz	1 pt	1 pt 8 oz	1 qt	1 qt 8 oz	1 qt 16 oz	1 qt 24 oz	2 qt	2 qt 8 oz	3 qt
Sour Cream	8 oz	1 pt	1 pt 8 oz	1 qt	1 qt 8 oz	1 qt 16 oz	1 qt 24 oz	2 qt	2 qt 8 oz	3 qt
Spinach, frozen, chopped	2 lb 8 oz	5 lb	7 lb 8 oz	10 lb	12 lb 8 oz	15 lb	17 lb 8 oz	20 lb	22 lb 8 oz	25 lb
Onion, chopped	1 T	2 T	¼ C	⅓ C	½ C	½ C	⅔ C	⅔ C	¾ C	1 C
Nutmeg	Dash	Dash	⅛ t	¼ t	½ t	½ t	¾ t	¾ t	1 t	1 t
Eggs, separated	3	6	9	12	15	18	21	24	27	30

Nutrient Analysis per serving

Protein:	5 g
Carbohydrate:	8 g
Fat:	11 g
Sodium:	236 mg
Kilocalories:	151

Procedure

1. Thaw the spinach.
2. Melt margarine. Add flour and salt and stir until smooth; cook for 2 minutes.
3. Add milk and sour cream. Blend over low heat until smooth, stirring constantly. Add spinach, nutmeg, onion, and egg yolks.
4. Beat egg whites until stiff. Fold into spinach mixture.
5. Pour into ungreased pan. Set in pan of hot water. Bake at 350°F 40 minutes or until set.

Note: If you do not have sour cream, buttermilk may be substituted.

SEASONED SUMMER SQUASH

CATEGORY: *Vegetable*   PORTION: ½ C, #8 dipper

INGREDIENTS	10	20	30	40	50	60	70	80	90	100
Margarine	1 oz	2 oz	3 oz	4 oz	5 oz	6 oz	7 oz	8 oz	9 oz	10 oz
Yellow Summer Squash, sliced	3 lb	6 lb	9 lb	12 lb	16 lb	19 lb	21 lb	25 lb	28 lb	32 lb
Onions, chopped	4 oz	8 oz	12 oz	1 lb	1 lb 8 oz	1 lb 12 oz	2 lb 2 oz	2 lb 6 oz	2 lb 8 oz	3 lb
Salt	½ t	1 t	1½ t	2 t	1 T	3½ t	4 t	1½ T	1¾ T	2 T
Pepper, white or black	Pinch	Dash	⅛ t	¼ t	½ t	½ t	¾ t	¾ t	1 t	1 t
Basil Leaves, or Ground Basil	½ t	1 t	1½ t	2 t	1 T	3½ t	4 t	1½ T	1¾ T	2 T
Oregano Leaves, or Ground Oregano	½ t	1 t	1½ t	2 t	1 T	3½ t	4 t	1½ T	1¾ T	2 T
Garlic Powder	Pinch	Dash	⅛ t	¼ t	¼ t	½ t	¾ t	¾ t	1 t	1 t
Parsley, chopped	½ T	1 T	2 T	3 T	4 T	4½ T	5 T	6 T	7 T	8 T

Nutrient Analysis per serving

Protein:	1 g
Carbohydrate:	6 g
Fat:	1 g
Sodium:	125 mg
Kilocalories:	41

Procedure

1. Melt margarine, add squash, onion, and seasonings.
2. Cover and cook until tender about 20 minutes.
3. Drain and stir in chopped parsley.

SQUASH CASSEROLE #1

CATEGORY: *Vegetable* **PORTION:** *½ C, #8 dipper*

INGREDIENTS	10	20	30	40	50	60	70	80	90	100
Yellow Squash	2 lb	4 lb	6 lb	8 lb	9 lb	11 lb	13 lb	15 lb	17 lb	18 lb
Margarine	2 oz	4 oz	6 oz	8 oz	1 lb	1 lb 2 oz	1 lb 4 oz	1 lb 6 oz	1 lb 8 oz	2 lb
Milk	2 oz	4 oz	8 oz	10 oz	12 oz	14 oz	1 pt	1 pt 2 oz	1 pt 4 oz	1 pt 6 oz
Onion, grated	¼ C	¾ C	1¼ C	1½ C	2 C	2¼ C	2¾ C	3¼ C	3½ C	4 C
Brown Sugar	1 T	1½ T	¼ C	⅓ C	½ C	½ C 1 T	½ C 1 T	⅔ C	¾ C	1 C
Salt	½ t	1 t	2 t	3 t	4 t	4½ t	5 t	6 t	7 t	8 t
Eggs	1	2	3	4	6	7	8	9	10	12
Cheddar Cheese Sauce	8 oz	1 pt 2 oz	1 pt 12 oz	1 qt 6 oz	1 qt 16 oz	2 qt	2 qt 2 oz	2 qt 16 oz	2 qt 24 oz	3 qt
Bread, torn in pieces	1¼ C	2½ C	4 C	5 C	6 C	7¼ C	8½ C	10 C	11 C	12 C

Nutrient Analysis per serving

Protein: 11 g
Carbohydrate: 5 g
Fat: 12 g
Sodium: 790 mg
Kilocalories: 260

Procedure

1. Cook squash and melt margarine in pan.
2. Beat eggs in bowl and set aside. Grate onion.
3. Measure milk, brown sugar, and salt. Mix well and add beaten eggs, grated onion, and melted margarine.
4. Drain the squash.
5. In buttered pans, place a layer of torn bread, a layer of squash, and a layer of cheese sauce.
6. Repeat all 3 layers and bake at 350°F for 30 minutes.

SQUASH CASSEROLE #2

CATEGORY: *Vegetable*   PORTION: ½ C, #8 dipper

INGREDIENTS	10	20	30	40	50	60	70	80	90	100
Yellow Squash, frozen, sliced	2 lb	4 lb	6 lb	8 lb	10 lb	12 lb	14 lb	16 lb	18 lb	20 lb
Salt	1 t	2 t	1 T	1 T	2 T	2 T	2 T	3 T	3 T	3 T
Sugar	1 t	2 t	1 T	1 T	2 T	2 T	2 T	3 T	3 T	3 T
Margarine, melted	1 oz	2 oz	3 oz	4 oz	5 oz	6 oz	7 oz	8 oz	9 oz	10 oz
Salt	¼ t	½ t	¾ t	1 t	1¼ t	1½ t	1¾ t	2 t	2¼ t	2½ t
Flour	1 oz	2 oz	3 oz	4 oz	5 oz	6 oz	7 oz	8 oz	9 oz	10 oz
Milk	1 pt 4 oz	1 qt 4 oz	1 qt 20 oz	2 qt 8 oz	2 qt 24 oz	3 qt 12 oz	1 gal	1 gal 16 oz	1 gal 32 oz	1 gal 64 oz
Pepper	½ t	1 t	1½ t	2 t	2½ t	1 T	1 T	1½ T	1½ T	2 T
Onion, fresh, chopped	8 oz	1 lb	1 lb 8 oz	2 lb	2 lb 8 oz	3 lb	3 lb 8 oz	4 lb	4 lb 8 oz	5 lb
American Cheese, shredded	8 oz	1 lb	1 lb 8 oz	2 lb	2 lb 8 oz	3 lb	3 lb 8 oz	4 lb	4 lb 8 oz	5 lb
Cracker Crumbs	4 oz	8 oz	12 oz	1 lb	1 lb 4 oz	1 lb 8 oz	1 lb 12 oz	2 lb	2 lb 4 oz	2 lb 8 oz

Nutrient Analysis per serving

Protein:	5 g
Carbohydrate:	11 g
Fat:	12 g
Sodium:	342 mg
Kilocalories:	176

Procedure

1. Cook squash in boiling, salted water with sugar for 15 minutes. Drain and set aside.
2. Combine margarine, salt, flour.
3. Stir in milk gradually. Heat over medium heat, stirring constantly until thickened.
4. Place squash in greased baking pan. Layer with pepper, onion, cheese, and sauce.
5. Sprinkle with cracker crumbs.
6. Bake in 350°F oven for 30 minutes or until hot and bubbly.

SWEET POTATO CASSEROLE

CATEGORY: *Vegetable*   PORTION: ½ C, #8 dipper

INGREDIENTS	10	20	30	40	50	60	70	80	90	100
Sweet Potatoes, drained	1 qt 6 oz	2 qt 12 oz	4 qt 2 oz	5 qt 8 oz	6 qt	7 qt 6 oz	8 qt 2 oz	11 qt	11 qt 8 oz	12 qt
Cinnamon, ground	½ t	1 t	1½ t	2 t	2½ t	3 t	3½ t	4 t	4½ t	5 t
Nutmeg	¼ t	½ t	¾ t	1 t	1¼ t	1½ t	1¾ t	2 t	2¼ t	2½ t
Eggs	1	2	3	4	5	6	7	8	9	10
Brown Sugar	¼ C	½ C	¾ C	1 C	1¼ C	1½ C	1¾ C	2 C	2¼ C	2½ C
Margarine, melted	2 oz	4 oz	6 oz	8 oz	10 oz	12 oz	14 oz	1 lb	1 lb 2 oz	1 lb 4 oz
Milk	2 T	¼ C	½ C	¾ C	1 C	1¼ C	1½ C	1¾ C	2 C	2¼ C

Nutrient Analysis per serving

Protein:	1 g
Carbohydrate:	29 g
Fat:	5 g
Sodium:	99 mg
Kilocalories:	172

Procedure

1. Combine potatoes, spices, and eggs in mixing bowl. Whip until fluffy.
2. Add enough of reserved liquid to make a light consistency.
3. Add brown sugar and margarine and whip.
4. Add milk.
5. Bake in 350°F oven for 45 minutes or until hot and bubbly.

CANDIED SWEET POTATOES

CATEGORY: *Vegetable*   PORTION: ½ C, #8 dipper

INGREDIENTS	10	20	30	40	50	60	70	80	90	100
Sweet Potatoes, fresh	4 lb	8 lb	12 lb	16 lb	20 lb	24 lb	28 lb	32 lb	36 lb	40 lb
Light Brown Sugar	6 oz	12 oz	1 lb	1 lb 6 oz	1 lb 12 oz	2 lb	2 lb 8 oz	2 lb 12 oz	3 lb	3 lb 2 oz
Margarine	2 oz	4 oz	6 oz	8 oz	10 oz	12 oz	14 oz	1 lb	1 lb 2 oz	1 lb 4 oz
Water	2 oz	4 oz	6 oz	8 oz	10 oz	12 oz	14 oz	1 lb	1 lb 2 oz	1 lb 4 oz
Salt	⅛ t	¼ t	½ t	¾ t	1 t	1⅛ t	1¼ t	1½ t	1¾ t	2 t

Nutrient Analysis per serving

Protein:	2 g
Carbohydrate:	62 g
Fat:	5 g
Sodium:	156 mg
Kilocalories:	300

Procedure

1. Steam or boil potatoes in skins until tender. Peel and cut in half.
2. Arrange potatoes in shallow baking pans.
3. Mix sugar, water, margarine, and salt and heat to boiling. Pour over potatoes. Bake at 400°F for 30 minutes.

BROILED TOMATOES

INGREDIENTS	10	20	30	40	50	60	70	80	90	100
Mayonnaise	½ C	1 C	1½ C	2 C	2½ C	3 C	3½ C	4 C	4½ C	5 C
Parmesan Cheese	½ C	1 C	1½ C	2 C	2½ C	3 C	3½ C	4 C	4½ C	5 C
Onion, fresh, minced	½ C	1 C	1½ C	2 C	2½ C	3 C	3½ C	4 C	4½ C	5 C
Parsley, fresh, minced	¼ C	⅓ C	½ C	¾ C	1 C	1 C	1¼ C	1⅓ C	1½ C	1¾ C
Tomatoes, medium, ripe, halved	5	10	15	20	25	30	35	40	45	50

Nutrient Analysis per serving

Protein:	3 g
Carbohydrate:	7 g
Fat:	5 g
Sodium:	162 mg
Kilocalories:	93

Procedure

1. Preheat broiler.
2. Combine all ingredients except tomatoes in small bowl and blend well.
3. Gently spread mixture about ¼ inch thick on tomatoes.
4. Broil 4 inches from heat source for 2 to 3 minutes or until lightly browned. (Watch carefully.)
5. Serve at once.

SCALLOPED TOMATOES

CATEGORY: *Vegetable*   PORTION: *½ C, #8 dipper*

INGREDIENTS	10	20	30	40	50	60	70	80	90	100
Tomatoes, canned	2 lb 8 oz	5 lb	7 lb 8 oz	10 lb	12 lb 8 oz	14 lb	16 lb 8 oz	18 lb	20 lb 8 oz	25 lb
Margarine, melted	2 oz	4 oz	6 oz	8 oz	10 oz	12 oz	14 oz	1 lb	1 lb 2 oz	1 lb 4 oz
Sugar	¼ C	⅓ C	½ C	¾ C	1 C	1¼ C	1⅓ C	1½ C	1¾ C	2 C
Bread, cubed	4 oz	6 oz	8 oz	12 oz	1 lb	1 lb 4 oz	1 lb 6 oz	1 lb 8 oz	1 lb 12 oz	2 lb

Nutrient Analysis per serving

Protein:	3 g
Carbohydrate:	18 g
Fat:	5 g
Sodium:	498 mg
Kilocalories:	128

Procedure

1. Add cubed bread, margarine, and sugar to tomatoes.
2. Pour into greased pans.
3. Baked at 350°F for 30 minutes or until hot and bubbly.

ITALIAN ZUCCHINI CASSEROLE

CATEGORY: *Vegetable*   PORTION: ½ C, #8 dipper

INGREDIENTS	10	20	30	40	50	60	70	80	90	100
Margarine	1 oz	2 oz	3 oz	4 oz	5 oz	6 oz	7 oz	8 oz	9 oz	10 oz
Zucchini, frozen	2 lb	4 lb	6 lb	8 lb	10 lb	12 lb	14 lb	16 lb	18 lb	20 lb
Salt	¼ t	½ t	¾ t	1 t	1½ t	1¾ t	2 t	2¼ t	2½ t	1 T
Garlic Powder	Dash	⅛ t	¼ t	½ t	¾ t	1 t	1¼ t	1½ t	1¾ t	2 t
Tomato Sauce	6 oz	12 oz	1 pt 2 oz	24 oz	1 qt	1 qt 6 oz	1 qt 12 oz	1 qt 16 oz	1 qt 24 oz	2 qt
Cheddar Cheese, grated	6 oz	12 oz	1 pt 2 oz	24 oz	1 qt	1 qt 6 oz	1 qt 12 oz	1 qt 16 oz	1 qt 24 oz	2 qt

Nutrient Analysis per serving

Protein:	4 g
Carbohydrate:	6 g
Fat:	6 g
Sodium:	386 mg
Kilocalories:	95

Procedure

1. Layer frozen zucchini in 12″ × 20″ steam-table pan.
2. Melt margarine and add salt, tomato sauce, and half of the cheddar cheese. Heat, stirring occasionally until the cheese is melted.
3. Pour sauce over zucchini and sprinkle with remaining cheese.
4. Bake at 325°F for 40 minutes.

CHEESE GRITS

CATEGORY: *Starch*   PORTION: ½ C, #8 dipper

INGREDIENTS	10	20	30	40	50	60	70	80	90	100
Salt	1 t	2 t	1 T	1½ T	2 T	2¼ T	2½ T	3 T	3½ T	4 T
Water	1 pt 4 oz	1 qt 6 oz	1 qt 24 oz	2 qt 12 oz	3 qt	3 qt 16 oz	4 qt 6 oz	4 qt 24 oz	5 qt 12 oz	6 qt
Grits	12 oz	1 lb 8 oz	2 lb 6 oz	3 lb	4 lb	4 lb 12 oz	5 lb 8 oz	6 lb 6 oz	7 lb	8 lb
Margarine	12 oz	1 lb 8 oz	2 lb 6 oz	3 lb	4 lb	4 lb 12 oz	5 lb 8 oz	6 lb 6 oz	7 lb	8 lb
Milk	12 oz	1 pt 8 oz	1 qt 6 oz	1 qt 16 oz	2 qt	2 qt 6 oz	2 qt 12 oz	3 qt 6 oz	3 qt 16 oz	4 qt
Eggs, beaten	2	5	7	10	12	14	17	19	22	24
Cheese, shredded	6 oz	12 oz	1 lb 4 oz	1 lb 8 oz	2 lb	2 lb 6 oz	2 lb 12 oz	3 lb 4 oz	3 lb 8 oz	4 lb

Nutrient Analysis per serving

Protein:	7 g
Carbohydrate:	10 g
Fat:	36 g
Sodium:	774 mg
Kilocalories:	400

Procedure

1. Add salt to water; bring to a boil.
2. Stir in grits slowly, keeping water at a brisk boil. Cover and cook slowly for 1 hour or until grits are soft, stirring occasionally.
3. Remove from heat; stir in margarine and milk.
4. Cool to lukewarm; beat in eggs and turn into greased casserole.
5. Bake at 350°F for 1 hour until dish is done.
6. Ten minutes before dish is done, sprinkle cheese over top.

HONEY CORNBREAD

INGREDIENTS	10	20	30	40	50	60	70	80	90	100
Corn Meal	8 oz	1 lb 2 oz	1 lb 12 oz	2 lb 6 oz	3 lb	3 lb 8 oz	4 lb 2 oz	4 lb 12 oz	5 lb 6 oz	6 lb
Flour, sifted	8 oz	1 lb 2 oz	1 lb 12 oz	2 lb 6 oz	3 lb	3 lb 8 oz	4 lb 2 oz	4 lb 12 oz	5 lb 6 oz	6 lb
Baking Powder	1 T	2 T	4 T	5 T	6 T	7 T	8 T	10 T	11 T	12 T
Salt	¾ t	1½ t	2½ t	3 t	4 t	5 t	6 t	7 t	7½ t	8 t
Eggs	1	2	3	3	4	4	5	6	7	8
Honey	⅓ C	¾ C	1 C	1¼ C	1½ C	1¾ C	2¼ C	2½ C	2¾ C	3 C
Fat, melted	2 oz	4 oz	5 oz	6 oz	8 oz	10 oz	12 oz	13 oz	14 oz	1 lb

Nutrient Analysis per serving

Protein:	5 g
Carbohydrate:	44 g
Fat:	6 g
Sodium:	267 mg
Kilocalories:	254

Procedure

1. Sift dry ingredients into bowl.
2. Add eggs, milk, and honey, stirring until combined. Fold in melted fat.
3. Bake in greased baking pans approximately 16″ × 10″ × 2″ in 400°F oven for 20 to 25 minutes.

OVEN RICE PILAF

INGREDIENTS	10	20	30	40	50	60	70	80	90	100
Rice	8 oz	1 lb	1 lb 8 oz	2 lb 6 oz	3 lb	3 lb 8 oz	4 lb	4 lb 8 oz	5 lb 6 oz	6 lb
Margarine, vegetable	4 oz	6 oz	8 oz	12 oz	1 lb	1 lb 4 oz	1 lb 6 oz	1 lb 8 oz	1 lb 12 oz	2 lb
Water	1 pt 8 oz	1 qt 16 oz	2 qt 12 oz	3 qt 6 oz	1 gal	1 gal 24 oz	1 gal 1 qt	1 gal 2 qt	1 gal 3 qt	2 gal
Salt	½ t	1 t	1½ t	2 t	3 t	5 t	5½ t	6 t	7 t	8 t
Green Pepper	4 oz	6 oz	8 oz	12 oz	1 lb	1 lb 4 oz	1 lb 6 oz	1 lb 8 oz	1 lb 12 oz	2 lb
Onion	2 oz	4 oz	6 oz	8 oz	10 oz	12 oz	14 oz	1 lb	1 lb 2 oz	1 lb 4 oz
Pimiento	2 oz	3 oz	4 oz	6 oz	8 oz	10 oz	11 oz	12 oz	14 oz	1 lb

Nutrient Analysis per serving

Protein:	2 g
Carbohydrate:	18 g
Fat:	6 g
Sodium:	218 mg
Kilocalories:	106

Procedure

1. Brown rice in margarine. Add water and salt. Cook for 30 minutes. Add green pepper, onion, and pimiento.
2. Cover tightly with aluminum foil and bake for 45 minutes in 350°F oven.

TEXAS RICE

CATEGORY: Starch   PORTION: ½ C, #8 scoop

INGREDIENTS	10	20	30	40	50	60	70	80	90	100
Onion, fresh, chopped	⅔ C	1⅓ C	2 C	2⅔ C	3 C	3⅔ C	4⅓ C	5 C	5⅔ C	6 C
Green Pepper, fresh, diced	⅔ C	1⅓ C	2 C	2⅔ C	3 C	3⅔ C	4⅓ C	5 C	5⅔ C	6 C
Margarine	2 oz	4 oz	6 oz	8 oz	10 oz	12 oz	14 oz	1 lb	1 lb 2 oz	1 lb 4 oz
Rice, cooked, hot	1 qt	2 qt	3 qt	1 gal	1 gal 1 qt	1 gal 2 qt	1 gal 3 qt	2 gal	2 gal 1 qt	2 gal 2 qt
Pimiento, diced	¼ C	½ C	¾ C	1 C	1¼ C	1½ C	1¾ C	2 C	2¼ C	2½ C
Salt	1 t	2 t	3 t	4 t	5 t	6 t	7 t	8 t	9 t	10 t

Nutrient Analysis per serving

Protein: 2 g
Carbohydrate: 21 g
Fat: 5 g
Sodium: 503 mg
Kilocalories: 135

Procedure

1. Prepare rice according to package directions.
2. Sauté onion and green pepper in margarine until tender-crisp.
3. Add onion mixture, pimiento, and salt to rice. Toss lightly.

Vegetables and Starch Dishes   163

CHAPTER 7   *Desserts*

BANANA SALAD DESSERT

INGREDIENTS	10	20	30	40	50	60	70	80	90	100
Bananas	5	10	15	20	25	30	35	40	45	50
Salad Dressing	6 oz	12 oz	18 oz	24 oz	1 qt	1 qt 6 oz	1 qt 12 oz	1 qt 18 oz	1 qt 24 oz	2 qt
Corn Flake Crumbs	6 oz	10 oz	1 lb	1 lb 4 oz	1 lb 8 oz	1 lb 14 oz	2 lb 3 oz	2 lb 8 oz	2 lb 12 oz	3 lb
Pineapple, crushed	12 oz	1 pt 8 oz	1 qt 4 oz	1 qt 16 oz	2 qt	2 qt 12 oz	2 qt 24 oz	3 qt	3 qt 12 oz	1 gal
Maraschino Cherries, whole	10	20	30	40	50	60	70	80	90	100

Nutrient Analysis per serving

Protein:	2 g
Carbohydrate:	34 g
Fat:	14 g
Sodium:	277 mg
Kilocalories:	266

Procedure

1. Slice bananas in half crosswise and lengthwise, making four pieces.
2. Roll bananas in salad dressing and place on lettuce leaf.
3. Sprinkle with corn flake crumbs and garnish with crushed pineapple and one whole cherry.

BISHOP'S CAKE

INGREDIENTS	10	20	30	40	50	60	70	80	90	100
Cake Mix, yellow	12 oz	1 lb 8 oz	2 lb 4 oz	3 lb 2 oz	3 lb 12 oz	4 lb 8 oz	5 lb 8 oz	6 lb 4 oz	7 lb	7 lb 8 oz
Whipped Topping, powdered	2 oz	4 oz	8 oz	10 oz	12 oz	1 lb	1 lb 2 oz	1 lb 4 oz	1 lb 8 oz	1 lb 12 oz
Pineapple, crushed, drained	10 oz	1 lb 4 oz	2 lb	2 lb 8 oz	3 lb 2 oz	4 lb	4 lb 6 oz	5 lb 2 oz	5 lb 4 oz	6 lb 4 oz
Maraschino Cherries	10	20	30	40	50	60	70	80	90	100

Nutrient Analysis per serving

Protein:	4 g
Carbohydrate:	58 g
Fat:	14 g
Sodium:	405 mg
Kilocalories:	377

Procedure

1. Prepare yellow cake mix according to directions on package.
2. Prepare whipped topping according to package directions.
3. Mix whipped topping and drained pineapple together.
4. Frost cake with pineapple topping mixture.
5. Cut into portions.
6. Place one cherry on each cake portion.

BUTTERMILK PIE

INGREDIENTS	10	20	30	40	50	60	70	80	90	100
Eggs	3	6	9	12	15	18	21	24	27	30
Sugar	12 oz	1 lb 8 oz	2 lb 4 oz	3 lb	3 lb 12 oz	4 lb 8 oz	5 lb 4 oz	6 lb	6 lb 12 oz	7 lb 8 oz
Flour	1 T	2 T	3 T	4 T	5 T	6 T	7 T	8 T	9 T	10 T
Salt	⅛ t	¼ t	⅓ t	½ t	½ t	¾ t	¾ t	1 t	1⅛ t	1¼ t
Buttermilk	6 oz	12 oz	1 pt 2 oz	1 pt 8 oz	1 pt 12 oz	1 qt	1 qt 8 oz	1 qt 16 oz	1 qt 24 oz	2 qt
Vanilla	¼ t	¾ t	1 t	1¼ t	1½ t	1¾ t	2¼ t	2½ t	2¾ t	3 t
Margarine	4 oz	8 oz	10 oz	12 oz	1 lb	1 lb 2 oz	1 lb 4 oz	1 lb 6 oz	1 lb 8 oz	1 lb 12 oz
10″ Pie Shells	1	2	3	4	5	6	7	8	9	10

Nutrient Analysis per serving

Protein: 4 g
Carbohydrate: 54 g
Fat: 21 g
Sodium: 364 mg
Kilocalories: 418

Procedure

1. Mix sugar, flour, and salt.
2. Beat eggs and add sugar mixture.
3. Add buttermilk and vanilla.
4. Add melted margarine.
5. Pour into 10″ pie shell.
6. Bake at 300°F, 30–35 minutes, or until knife inserted 1 inch from edge of filling comes out clean.

CHERRY DELIGHT

INGREDIENTS	10	20	30	40	50	60	70	80	90	100
Cream Cheese	4 oz	10 oz	1 lb	1 lb 4 oz	1 lb 10 oz	2 lb	2 lb 4 oz	2 lb 10 oz	3 lb	3 lb 4 oz
Sugar, powdered	⅔ C	1⅓ C	2 C	2⅔ C	3⅓ C	4 C	4⅔ C	5⅓ C	6 C	6⅔ C
Topping Mix, vanilla	2 oz	4 oz	6 oz	8 oz	10 oz	12 oz	14 oz	1 lb	1 lb 2 oz	1 lb 4 oz
Graham Crackers, crushed	½ C	1 C	1½ C	2 C	2½ C	3 C	3½ C	4 C	4½ C	5 C
Sugar	2 T	¼ C	6 T	½ C	10 T	¾ C	14 T	1 C	1 C 2 T	1¼ C
Margarine	2 oz	4 oz	6 oz	8 oz	10 oz	12 oz	14 oz	1 lb	1 lb 2 oz	1 lb 4 oz
Pie Filling, cherry	1 pt 4 oz	1 qt 8 oz	3 pt 12 oz	2 qt 16 oz	3 qt	1 gal	1 gal 1 pt	1 gal 1 qt	1 gal 2 qt	1 gal 3 qt

Nutrient Analysis per serving

Protein:	2 g
Carbohydrate:	37 g
Fat:	16 g
Sodium:	193 mg
Kilocalories:	297

Procedure

1. Cream cheese and sugar.
2. Whip topping; add to creamed mixture.
3. Blend ingredients; form crust.
4. Pour creamed mixture into graham cracker crust.
5. Top with pie filling; chill.

CHEWY BARS

INGREDIENTS	10	20	30	40	50	60	70	80	90	100
Cake Mix, yellow	8 oz	1 lb	1 lb 8 oz	2 lb	2 lb 8 oz	3 lb	3 lb 8 oz	4 lb	4 lb 8 oz	5 lb
Brown Sugar	2 oz	4 oz	6 oz	8 oz	10 oz	12 oz	14 oz	1 lb	1 lb 2 oz	1 lb 4 oz
Margarine	1 oz	2 oz	3 oz	4 oz	5 oz	6 oz	7 oz	8 oz	9 oz	10 oz
Corn Syrup	1 T	2 T	3 T	4 T	5 T	6 T	7 T	8 T	9 T	10 T
Chocolate Chips	¼ C	½ C	¾ C	1 C	1¼ C	1½ C	1¾ C	2 C	2¼ C	2½ C
Walnuts, chopped	½ C	1 C	1½ C	2 C	2½ C	3 C	3½ C	4 C	4½ C	5 C
Egg	1	2	3	4	5	6	7	8	9	10
Water	1 T	2 T	3 T	4 T	5 T	6 T	7 T	8 T	9 T	10 T
Flour	1 oz	2 oz	3 oz	4 oz	5 oz	6 oz	7 oz	8 oz	9 oz	10 oz

Nutrient Analysis per serving

Protein:	3 g
Carbohydrate:	25 g
Fat:	10 g
Sodium:	130 mg
Kilocalories:	196

Procedure

1. In a small bowl, blend all ingredients well.
2. Spread in greased shallow pan.
3. Bake at 350°F 25 to 30 minutes. Cool and cut into bars.

COCONUT PIE

INGREDIENTS	10	20	30	40	50	60	70	80	90	100
Margarine	2 oz	4 oz	8 oz	10 oz	12 oz	14 oz	1 lb	1 lb 4 oz	1 lb 6 oz	1 lb 8 oz
Sugar	8 oz	1 lb 4 oz	1 lb 12 oz	2 lb 8 oz	3 lb	3 lb 8 oz	4 lb 4 oz	4 lb 12 oz	5 lb 8 oz	6 lb
Eggs	2	4	6	10	12	14	16	18	22	25
Nonfat Dry Milk, reconstituted	8 oz	1 pt 2 oz	1 pt 12 oz	1 qt 6 oz	1 qt 16 oz	1 qt 24 oz	2 qt	2 qt 12 oz	2 qt 24 oz	3 qt
Flour, self-rising	¼ C	½ C	¾ C	1 C	1½ C	1¾ C	2 C	2½ C	2¾ C	3 C
Coconut, flaked	4 oz	8 oz	12 oz	1 lb	1 lb 4 oz	1 lb 8 oz	1 lb 12 oz	2 lb	2 lb 4 oz	2 lb 8 oz

Nutrient Analysis per serving

Protein:	3 g
Carbohydrate:	39 g
Fat:	12 g
Sodium:	187 mg
Kilocalories:	276

Procedure

1. Cream margarine and sugar.
2. Add one egg at a time, mixing well after each addition.
3. Add milk and flour. Blend well.
4. Add coconut.
5. Pour into lightly greased pie tins.
6. Bake at 350°F for 45 minutes, or until set.

CRUMB COOKIES

INGREDIENTS	10	20	30	40	50	60	70	80	90	100
Margarine	4 oz	8 oz	12 oz	1 lb	1 lb 4 oz	1 lb 8 oz	1 lb 12 oz	2 lb	2 lb 4 oz	2 lb 8 oz
Sugar	¾ C	1½ C	2¼ C	3¼ C	4 C	4¾ C	5½ C	6¼ C	7¼ C	8 C
Egg	½	1	2	3	4	4½	5	6	7	8
Flour	¾ C	1½ C	2¼ C	3¼ C	4 C	4¾ C	5½ C	6¼ C	7¼ C	8 C
Baking Soda	½ t	1 t	1½ t	1¾ t	2 t	2½ t	3 t	3½ t	3¾ t	4 t
Cream of Tartar	½ t	1 t	1½ t	1¾ t	2 t	2½ t	3 t	3½ t	3¾ t	4 t
Salt	pinch	⅛ t	¼ t	⅓ t	½ t	½ t	⅔ t	¾ t	¾ t	1 t
Cookie or Cake Crumbs	6 oz	12 oz	1 lb 2 oz	1 lb 8 oz	2 lb	2 lb 6 oz	2 lb 12 oz	2 lb 16 oz	2 lb 24 oz	4 lb
Raisins	⅓ C	⅔ C	1 C	2 C	2⅓ C	2¾ C	3 C	3¾ C	4⅓ C	4⅔ C
Oats	6 oz	12 oz	1 lb 2 oz	1 lb 8 oz	2 lb	2 lb 6 oz	2 lb 12 oz	2 lb 16 oz	2 lb 24 oz	4 lb

Nutrient Analysis per serving

Protein:	5 g
Carbohydrate:	47 g
Fat:	12 g
Sodium:	253 mg
Kilocalories:	319

Procedure

1. Blend together margarine, sugar, and eggs.
2. Add flour, baking soda, cream of tartar, and salt.
3. Mix in cookie crumbs, raisins, and oats.
4. Use #40 scoop and flatten on greased pan.
5. Bake at 350°F until brown, approximately 10–12 minutes.

DREAM SALAD

CATEGORY: *Dessert or Salad*   PORTION: $\frac{1}{3}$ *C, #12 dipper*

INGREDIENTS	10	20	30	40	50	60	70	80	90	100
Whipped Topping	4 oz	8 oz	10 oz	12 oz	1 pt	1 pt 4 oz	1 pt 8 oz	1 pt 10 oz	1 pt 12 oz	1 qt
Gelatin (any flavor)	4 oz	8 oz	10 oz	12 oz	1 pt	1 pt 4 oz	1 pt 8 oz	1 pt 10 oz	1 pt 12 oz	1 qt
Pineapple, crushed	6 oz	12 oz	1 pt	1 pt 8 oz	1 qt	1 qt 6 oz	1 qt 12 oz	1 qt 16 oz	1 qt 24 oz	2 qt
Cranberry Sauce	6 oz	12 oz	1 pt	1 pt 8 oz	1 qt	1 qt 6 oz	1 qt 12 oz	1 qt 16 oz	1 qt 24 oz	2 qt
Marshmallows, mini	2 oz	3 oz	4 oz	6 oz	8 oz	10 oz	11 oz	12 oz	14 oz	1 lb

Nutrient Analysis per serving

Protein:	1 g
Carbohydrate:	24 g
Fat:	4 g
Sodium:	37 mg
Kilocalories:	138

Procedure

1. Cut cranberry sauce in very small chunks.
2. Whip dry gelatin and whipped topping together.
3. Fold in marshmallows, drained pineapple, and cranberry sauce.
4. Chill 2-3 hours before serving.

FROZEN AMBROSIA

CATEGORY: *Dessert*   PORTION: *2" square*

INGREDIENTS	10	20	30	40	50	60	70	80	90	100
Graham Cracker Crumbs	4 oz	8 oz	1 lb	1 lb 4 oz	1 lb 8 oz	1 lb 12 oz	2 lb	2 lb 8 oz	2 lb 12 oz	3 lb
Margarine	2 oz	4 oz	8 oz	10 oz	12 oz	14 oz	1 lb	1 lb 4 oz	1 lb 6 oz	1 lb 16 oz
Fruit Mix, canned	1 lb 2 oz	2 lb 6 oz	3 lb 8 oz	4 lb 8 oz	3 qt	3 qt 8 oz	4 qt	4 qt 8 oz	5 qt	6 qt
Whipped Topping	12 oz	1 pt 10 oz	1 qt 6 oz	1 qt 12 oz	2 qt	2 qt 12 oz	3 qt	3 qt 4 oz	3 qt 12 oz	1 gal

Nutrient Analysis per serving

Protein:	1 g
Carbohydrate:	19 g
Fat:	9 g
Sodium:	98 mg
Kilocalories:	162

Procedure

1. Mix graham cracker crumbs with margarine. Make crust in bottom of pan using half of the crumb mixture.
2. Combine drained fruit mix and whipped topping.
3. Put half of mixture on crust and sprinkle with crumbs.
4. Add remaining fruit mixture and sprinkle with remainder of crumbs. The top layer should be graham crumbs.
5. Freeze the day before serving.

FROZEN PUDDING SQUARE

CATEGORY: Dessert   PORTION: 2½" square, ¼ C peaches

INGREDIENTS	10	20	30	40	50	60	70	80	90	100
Instant Pudding Mix, vanilla or pistachio	6 oz	12 oz	18 oz	24 oz	1 lb 12 oz	2 lb	2 lb 8 oz	2 lb 12 oz	3 lb	4 lb
Milk	1 pt 4 oz	2 pt 8 oz	2 qt	2 qt 16 oz	3 qt 4 oz	3 qt 24 oz	1 gal 8 oz	1 gal 1 qt	1 gal 2 qt	1 gal 3 qt
Whipped Topping, frozen, thawed	6 oz	12 oz	1 pt 4 oz	1 pt 8 oz	1 qt	1 qt 4 oz	1 qt 12 oz	1 qt 16 oz	1 qt 24 oz	2 qt
Peaches, sliced	1 lb 8 oz	3 lb	4 lb	6 lb	7 lb	8 lb	10 lb	11 lb	13 lb	14 lb

Nutrient Analysis per serving

Protein:	6 g
Carbohydrate:	34 g
Fat:	8 g
Sodium:	359 mg
Kilocalories:	237

Procedure

1. Beat milk and mix slowly for 2 minutes.
2. Blend whipped topping into pudding. Pour into pan(s). Freeze 4 hours or overnight.
3. Cut pudding into 2" × 2½" squares with ¼ C peaches on top.

HONEY BEE AMBROSIA

CATEGORY: Dessert   PORTION: ½ C, #8 dipper

INGREDIENTS	10	20	30	40	50	60	70	80	90	100
Orange Sections, canned	16 oz	1 qt	1 qt 16 oz	2 qt	3 qt	3 qt 16 oz	4 qt	5 qt	5 qt 16 oz	6 qt
Bananas, sliced	8 oz	1 lb	1 lb 8 oz	2 lb	3 lb	3 lb 8 oz	4 lb	4 lb 8 oz	5 lb	6 lb
Orange Juice	4 oz	8 oz	12 oz	1 pt	1 pt 8 oz	1 pt 12 oz	1 qt	1 qt 4 oz	1 qt 8 oz	1 qt 16 oz
Honey	2 oz	4 oz	6 oz	8 oz	12 oz	14 oz	1 pt	1 pt 2 oz	1 pt 4 oz	1 pt 8 oz
Lemon Juice, fresh	1 oz	2 oz	4 oz	5 oz	6 oz	7 oz	8 oz	10 oz	11 oz	12 oz
Coconut, flaked	2 T	3 T	4 T	5 T	6 T	8 T	10 T	11 T	12 T	14 T

Nutrient Analysis per serving

Protein:	1 g
Carbohydrate:	18 g
Fat:	1 g
Sodium:	6 mg
Kilocalories:	74

Procedure

1. Drain orange sections and place in serving bowl.
2. Peel bananas; cut thin slices in a bowl.
3. Toss fruits.
4. Blend orange juice, honey, and lemon juice; pour over fruits. Sprinkle with coconut.

MARSHMALLOW SQUARE

CATEGORY: Dessert   PORTION: 2" square

INGREDIENTS	10	20	30	40	50	60	70	80	90	100
Margarine, melted	1 oz	2 oz	3 oz	4 oz	5 oz	6 oz	7 oz	8 oz	9 oz	10 oz
Marshmallows	4 oz	8 oz	12 oz	1 lb	1 lb 2 oz	1 lb 4 oz	1 lb 8 oz	2 lb	2 lb 4 oz	2 lb 8 oz
Rice Krispies	2 C	4 C	6 C	8 C	10 C	12 C	14 C	16 C	18 C	20 C

Nutrient Analysis per serving

Protein:	0 g
Carbohydrate:	14 g
Fat:	2 g
Sodium:	99 mg
Kilocalories:	75

Procedure

1. Melt margarine, add marshmallows and cook, stirring constantly, until marshmallows are melted and mixture is syruplike.
2. Add Rice Krispies and stir until coated.
3. Spread warm mixture in buttered pans.
4. Press into an even layer.
5. Cool and cut in 2" squares.

MOCK ENGLISH TRIFLE

CATEGORY: Dessert   *PORTION: 2" square*

INGREDIENTS	10	20	30	40	50	60	70	80	90	100
Cake Crumbs, leftover	1 lb 2 oz	2 lb 4 oz	2 lb 24 oz	3 lb 2 oz	4 lb 4 oz	5 lb 6 oz	6 lb 8 oz	7 lb 12 oz	5 qt 8 oz	6 qt
Gelatin, cherry	12 oz	1 lb 8 oz	2 lb 4 oz	3 lb	4 lb 8 oz	4 lb 12 oz	6 lb	6 lb 12 oz	7 lb 8 oz	9 lb
Vanilla Pudding or No Bake Custard Mix	8 oz	1 lb 4 oz	1 lb 12 oz	2 lb 6 oz	3 lb	3 lb 8 oz	4 lb 4 oz	4 lb 12 oz	4 lb 6 oz	6 lb
Maraschino Cherries	10	20	30	40	50	60	70	80	90	100

Nutrient Analysis per serving

Protein: 7 g
Carbohydrate: 67 g
Fat: 11 g
Sodium: 656 mg
Kilocalories: 404

Procedure

1. Line baking pan(s) with pieces of cake, broken to cover bottom evenly.
2. Prepare gelatin according to package directions and pour over the cake crumbs. Cover, refrigerate, and set.
3. Prepare pudding according to package directions.
4. Spread evenly over set jello.
5. Top with cherry for each serving.
6. Cut into 2" × 2" squares and serve.

PEACHY CREAM PUDDING

CATEGORY: *Dessert*   PORTION: ½ C, #8 dipper

INGREDIENTS	10	20	30	40	50	60	70	80	90	100
Instant Pudding Mix, vanilla	4 oz	8 oz	12 oz	1 lb	1 lb 6 oz	1 lb 10 oz	1 lb 12 oz	2 lb 2 oz	2 lb 6 oz	2 lb 12 oz
Whipped Topping Mix	1 oz	2 oz	3 oz	4 oz	6 oz	7 oz	8 oz	9 oz	10 oz	12 oz
Peaches, cut and drained	16 oz	1 qt	1 qt 24 oz	2 qt 16 oz	3 qt	3 qt 16 oz	4 qt	4 pt 24 oz	5 qt 16 oz	6 qt

Nutrient Analysis per serving

Protein:	4 g
Carbohydrate:	30 g
Fat:	4 g
Sodium:	330 mg
Kilocalories:	179

Procedure

1. Prepare pudding according to package directions. Cool.
2. Prepare the whipped topping and fold into pudding.
3. Mix in the peaches and chill.

QUICK COOKIES

INGREDIENTS	10	20	30	40	50	60	70	80	90	100
Flour, self-rising	8 oz	1 lb	1 lb 8 oz	2 lb	2 lb 8 oz	3 lb	3 lb 8 oz	4 lb	4 lb 8 oz	5 lb
Shortening	2 oz	4 oz	8 oz	12 oz	1 lb	1 lb 2 oz	1 lb 4 oz	1 lb 8 oz	1 lb 12 oz	2 lb
Sugar	4 oz	8 oz	12 oz	1 lb	1 lb 4 oz	1 lb 8 oz	1 lb 12 oz	2 lb	2 lb 4 oz	2 lb 8 oz
Instant Pudding Mix, vanilla	2 oz	4 oz	6 oz	8 oz	10 oz	12 oz	14 oz	1 lb	1 lb 2 oz	1 lb 4 oz
Eggs	2	3	5	6	8	10	11	13	14	16

Nutrient Analysis per serving

Protein:	3 g
Carbohydrate:	31 g
Fat:	7 g
Sodium:	309 mg
Kilocalories:	200

Procedure

1. Mix flour, shortening, sugar, and vanilla pudding and eggs together well.
2. Drop by #40 scoop onto a greased cookie sheet.
3. Bake at 300°F until lightly browned, approximately 10–12 minutes.

Variations:
Peanut Butter: Add ⅔ C peanut butter per 100 portions.
Chocolate Chip: Add 2¾ C chocolate chips per 100 portions.
Sugar: Sprinkle sugar on top of cookies before baking.

ROCKY ROAD PUDDING

CATEGORY: *Dessert*   PORTION: ⅓ *C, # 16 dipper*

INGREDIENTS	10	20	30	40	50	60	70	80	90	100
Instant Pudding Mix, chocolate	8 oz	1 lb	1 lb 8 oz	2 lb	2 lb 4 oz	2 lb 12 oz	3 lb 4 oz	4 lb	4 lb 4 oz	4 lb 8 oz
Marshmallows, mini	6 oz	12 oz	1 lb 2 oz	1 lb 8 oz	1 qt	1 qt 6 oz	1 qt 12 oz	1 qt 1 pt	1 qt 24 oz	2 qt
Coconut, shredded	1 T	1½ T	3 T	2½ T	4 T	3 T	5½ T	6 T	7 T	8 T

Nutrient Analysis per serving

Protein:	4 g
Carbohydrate:	47 g
Fat:	6 g
Sodium:	81 mg
Kilocalories:	244

Procedure

1. Prepare pudding according to package directions.
2. Fold in marshmallows.
3. Portion into individual dishes.
4. Garnish with shredded coconut.

INGREDIENTS	10	20	30	40	50	60	70	80	90	100
Margarine	½ C	1 C	1½ C	2 C	2½ C	3 C	3½ C	4 C	4½ C	5 C
Sugar, granulated	¾ C	1½ C	2¼ C	3 C	3¾ C	4½ C	5¼ C	6 C	6¾ C	7½ C
Egg	1	2	3	4	5	6	7	8	9	10
Vanilla	1 t	2 t	3 t	4 t	5 t	6 t	7 t	8 t	9 t	10 t
Flour	1½ C	3 C	4½ C	6 C	7½ C	9 C	10½ C	12 C	13½ C	15 C
Baking Powder	1 t	2 t	3 t	4 t	5 t	6 t	7 t	8 t	9 t	10 t
Salt	¼ t	½ t	¾ t	1 t	1¼ t	1½ t	1¾ t	2 t	2¼ t	2½ t

Nutrient Analysis per serving

Protein:	2 g
Carbohydrate:	28 g
Fat:	9 g
Sodium:	200 mg
Kilocalories:	211

Procedure

1. Cream margarine and sugar until well blended. Beat in egg and vanilla, mixing well.
2. Sift dry ingredients together. Add this to the creamed mixture. Chill at least two hours, then roll and cut on floured surface.
3. Place on a greased cookie sheet. Bake at 400°F until firm, but not brown, approximately 10-12 minutes.

INGREDIENTS	10	20	30	40	50	60	70	80	90	100
Cake Mix, spice	12 oz	1 lb 8 oz	2 lb 4 oz	3 lb	3 lb 12 oz	4 lb 8 oz	5 lb	5 lb 12 oz	6 lb 8 oz	7 lb 4 oz
Tomato Juice	6 oz	12 oz	1 pt 2 oz	1 pt 8 oz	1 pt 14 oz	1 qt 4 oz	1 qt 10 oz	1 qt 16 oz	1 qt 24 oz	2 qt
Raisins	⅓ C	⅔ C	1 C	1⅓ C	1⅔ C	2 C	2⅓ C	2⅔ C	3 C	3⅓ C

Nutrient Analysis per serving

Protein:	2 g
Carbohydrate:	31 g
Fat:	4 g
Sodium:	293 mg
Kilocalories:	169

Procedure

1. Prepare cake batter according to package directions, substituting tomato juice for water.
2. Fold in raisins.
3. Bake according to package directions.

SPICY FRUIT COMPOTE

CATEGORY: Dessert   PORTION: ½ C, ladle

INGREDIENTS	10	20	30	40	50	60	70	80	90	100
Pineapple Tidbits, in natural juice	16 oz	1 qt	1 qt 16 oz	2 qt	2 qt 16 oz	3 qt	3 qt 16 oz	4 qt	4 qt 16 oz	5 qt
Pears, water-packed, sliced	16 oz	1 qt	1 qt 16 oz	2 qt	2 qt 16 oz	3 qt	3 qt 16 oz	4 qt	4 qt 16 oz	5 qt
Lemon Juice	¼ C	½ C	¾ C	1 C	1¼ C	1½ C	1¾ C	2 C	2¼ C	2½ C
Cloves, ground	½ t	¾ t	1 t	1¼ t	1½ t	2 t	2½ t	2¾ t	3 t	4 t
Cinnamon, ground	1¼ t	2½ t	3½ t	4 t	5 t	2 T	2½ T	3 T	3½ T	4 T
Oranges, peeled and sectioned	2	4	6	8	10	12	14	16	18	20

Nutrient Analysis per serving

Protein:	0 g
Carbohydrate:	16 g
Fat:	0 g
Sodium:	2.9 mg
Kilocalories:	69

Procedure

1. In pot combine fruit, undrained, with lemon juice.
2. Add spices to fruit mixture. Bring to boil. Reduce heat; cover and simmer 8–10 minutes. Stir occasionally. Remove from heat.
3. Add orange sections. Refrigerate overnight.

STRABERRY HASH

CATEGORY: Dessert   *PORTION: ½ C, #8 dipper*

INGREDIENTS	10	20	30	40	50	60	70	80	90	100
Pineapple, crushed	1 pt	1 qt	1 qt 16 oz	2 qt	2 qt 16 oz	3 qt	3 qt 16 oz	4 qt	4 qt 16 oz	5 qt
Mandarin Oranges	1 pt	1 qt	1 qt 16 oz	2 qt	2 qt 16 oz	3 qt	3 qt 16 oz	4 qt	4 qt 16 oz	5 qt
Marshmallows, mini	2 oz	4 oz	8 oz	10 oz	12 oz	1 lb	1 lb 2 oz	1 lb 4 oz	1 lb 6 oz	1 lb 8 oz
Strawberry Glaze	4 oz	8 oz	14 oz	1 lb 2 oz	24 oz	1 qt	1 qt 2 oz	1 qt 6 oz	1 qt 12 oz	1 qt 16 oz

Nutrient Analysis per serving

Protein: 0 g
Carbohydrate: 24 g
Fat: 0 g
Sodium: 9 mg
Kilocalories: 90

Procedure

1. Mix fruit and marshmallows together.
2. Pour glaze over fruit and mix. Refrigerate until serving time.

CHAPTER 8   *Sauces, Supplements, and Toppings*

GLAZE FOR HAM LOAF

CATEGORY: Condiment   PORTION: 2 T

INGREDIENTS	10	20	30	40	50	60	70	80	90	100
Ketchup	¼ C	¾ C	1 C	1½ C	1¾ C	2¼ C	2½ C	3 C	3¼ C	3¾ C
Mustard, dry	Pinch	Dash	⅛ t	¼ t	¼ t	⅓ t	⅓ t	½ t	⅔ t	⅔ t
Brown Sugar	¼ C	⅓ C	½ C	⅔ C	¾ C	1 C	1½ C	1⅓ C	1½ C	1⅔ C
Pineapple, crushed	1 C	2 C	3 C	4 C	5 C	6 C	7 C	8 C	9 C	12 C

Nutrient Analysis per serving

Protein:	0 g
Carbohydrate:	9 g
Fat:	0 g
Sodium:	101 mg
Kilocalories:	38

Procedure

1. Combine ketchup, dry mustard, brown sugar, and crushed pineapple for glaze.

CARAMEL SAUCE

CATEGORY: Sauce   PORTION: 2 oz

INGREDIENTS	10	20	30	40	50	60	70	80	90	100
Butter or Margarine	1 oz	2 oz	3 oz	4 oz	5 oz	6 oz	7 oz	8 oz	9 oz	10 oz
Flour, all-purpose	2 T	¼ C	⅓ C	½ C	⅔ C	¾ C	¾ C	1 C	1 C 2 T	1¼ C
Half and Half	12 oz	1 pt 8 oz	1 qt 4 oz	1 qt 16 oz	1 qt 28 oz	2 qt 8 oz	2 qt 20 oz	3 qt	3 qt 12 oz	3 qt 24 oz
Light Brown Sugar, packed	6 oz	12 oz	1 lb 2 oz	1 lb 8 oz	1 lb 14 oz	2 lb 4 oz	2 lb 10 oz	3 lb	3 lb 6 oz	3 lb 12 oz
Sugar, granulated	6 oz	12 oz	1 lb 2 oz	1 lb 8 oz	1 lb 14 oz	2 lb 4 oz	2 lb 10 oz	3 lb	3 lb 6 oz	3 lb 12 oz
Salt	¼ t	½ t	¾ t	1 t	1¼ t	1½ t	1¾ t	2 t	2¼ t	2½ t

Nutrient Analysis per serving

Protein:	0 g
Carbohydrate:	14 g
Fat:	2 g
Sodium:	41 mg
Kilocalories:	79

Procedure

1. Melt margarine in saucepan and stir in flour until blended.
2. Gradually stir in half and half; cook, stirring constantly, until mixture is thickened and smooth.
3. Add brown sugar, sugar, and salt; stir until mixed.
4. Serve warm or refrigerate to serve cold.

HOT BUTTERSCOTCH SAUCE

CATEGORY: *Sauce*   PORTION: *2 oz*

INGREDIENTS	10	20	30	40	50	60	70	80	90	100
Brown Sugar, packed	1 lb	2 lb	3 lb	4 lb	5 lb	6 lb	7 lb	8 lb	9 lb	10 lb
Half and Half	4 oz	8 oz	1 pt	1 pt 4 oz	1 pt 8 oz	2 pt	2 pt 4 oz	2 pt 10 oz	3 pt	3 pt 4 oz
Margarine	2 oz	4 oz	6 oz	8 oz	10 oz	12 oz	14 oz	1 lb	1 lb 2 oz	1 lb 4 oz
Light Corn Syrup	1/3 C	2/3 C	1 C	1 1/3 C	1 2/3 C	2 C	2 1/3 C	2 2/3 C	3 C	3 1/3 C

Nutrient Analysis per serving

Protein:	0 g
Carbohydrate:	20 g
Fat:	2 g
Sodium:	32 mg
Kilocalories:	102

Procedure

1. In saucepan over medium heat, heat brown sugar, half and half, margarine, and corn syrup to boiling, stirring occasionally.
2. Serve warm over ice cream, cake, or custard.

TERIYAKI SAUCE

INGREDIENTS	10	20	30	40	50	60	70	80	90	100
Soy Sauce	½ C	1 C	1½ C	2 C	3 C	3½ C	4 C	4½ C	5 C	6 C
Brown Sugar	2 oz	4 oz	6 oz	8 oz	10 oz	12 oz	14 oz	1 lb	1 lb 2 oz	1 lb 4 oz
Garlic Powder	¾ t	1½ t	2¼ t	1 T	1½ T	1¾ T	2 T	2½ T	2¾ T	3 T
Ginger	¾ t	1½ t	2¼ t	1 T	1½ T	1¾ T	2 T	2½ T	2¾ T	3 T

Nutrient Analysis per serving

Protein:	1 g
Carbohydrate:	6 g
Fat:	0 g
Sodium:	824 mg
Kilocalories:	31

Procedure

1. Combine all ingredients.
2. May be used to marinate a variety of meats, fish, or poultry.

VELOUTÉ SAUCE
FOR TURKEY PIE WITH CORNBREAD TOPPING

CATEGORY: Sauce   PORTION: per serving

INGREDIENTS	10	20	30	40	50	60	70	80	90	100
Margarine	10 oz	1 lb 4 oz	2 lb 4 oz	2 lb 8 oz	3 lb 2 oz	3 lb 12 oz	4 lb 6 oz	5 lb 6 oz	5 lb 10 oz	6 lb 4 oz
Flour	10 oz	1 lb 4 oz	2 lb 4 oz	2 lb 8 oz	3 lb 2 oz	3 lb 12 oz	4 lb 6 oz	5 lb 6 oz	5 lb 10 oz	6 lb 4 oz
Chicken Stock, hot	1 gal	2 gal	3 gal	4 gal	5 gal	6 gal	7 gal	8 gal	9 gal	10 gal

Nutrient Analysis per serving

Protein:	1 g
Carbohydrate:	10 g
Fat:	10 g
Sodium:	110 mg
Kilocalories:	137

Procedure

1. Melt butter in sauce pan. Add flour and stir to make a smooth roux. Cook roux slowly for about 5 minutes. Do not brown.
2. Slowly whip in stock until thickened and smooth. Cook slowly, stirring frequently, for about 30 minutes.
3. Strain and reserve for use in recipe.

BANANA MILKSHAKE

CATEGORY: Supplement   PORTION: 8 oz

INGREDIENTS	10	20	30	40	50	60	70	80	90	100
Nonfat Dry Milk	4 oz	8 oz	1 lb	1 lb 4 oz	1 lb 8 oz	1 lb 12 oz	2 lb 2 oz	2 lb 8 oz	2 lb 12 oz	3 lb
Water	1 qt 8 oz	2 qt 16 oz	3 qt 24 oz	1 gal 1 qt	1 gal 2 qt	1 gal 3 qt	2 gal 24 oz	2 gal 2 qt	2 gal 3 qt	3 gal 16 oz
Bananas, medium, mashed	3	6	9	12	15	18	21	24	27	30
Ice Cream	1 qt	1 qt 16 oz	2 qt	3 qt	1 gal	1 gal 24 oz	1 gal 1 qt	1 gal 2 qt	1 gal 3 qt	2 gal
Eggs	6	12	18	24	30	36	42	48	54	60

Nutrient Analysis per serving

Protein:	10 g
Carbohydrate:	24 g
Fat:	3 g
Sodium:	252 mg
Kilocalories:	206

Procedure

1. Combine all ingredients in mixing bowl and mix until smooth.
2. Portion into 8 oz servings. Serve immediately.

CHOCOLATE MILKSHAKE

CATEGORY: *Supplement*   PORTION: *8 oz*

INGREDIENTS	10	20	30	40	50	60	70	80	90	100
Nonfat Dry Milk	8 oz	1 lb	1 lb 8 oz	2 lb	2 lb 8 oz	3 lb	3 lb 8 oz	4 lb	4 lb 8 oz	5 lb
Water	1 qt 24 oz	3 qt 16 oz	1 gal 1 qt	1 gal 3 qt	2 gal 1 qt	2 gal 2 qt	3 gal 8 oz	3 gal 2 qt	3 gal 3 qt	4 gal 24 oz
Ice Cream, vanilla	1 pt 8 oz	1 qt 16 oz	2 qt	3 qt	1 gal	1 gal 24 oz	1 gal 1 qt	1 gal 2 qt	1 gal 3 qt	2 gal
Chocolate Syrup	10 oz	1 pt 4 oz	1 qt	1 qt 8 oz	1 qt 16 oz	1 qt 24 oz	2 qt	2 qt 16 oz	2 qt 24 oz	3 qt

Nutrient Analysis per serving

Protein: 10 g
Carbohydrate: 24 g
Fat: 3 g
Sodium: 152 mg
Kilocalories: 206

Procedure

1. Combine all ingredients in mixing bowl. Mix until smooth.
2. Portion into 8 oz servings. Serve immediately.

FORTIFIED MILK

CATEGORY: *Supplement*   PORTION: *8 oz*

INGREDIENTS	10	20	30	40	50	60	70	80	90	100
Milk, 2%	2 qt	1 gal	1 gal 2 qt	2 gal	2 gal 2 qt	3 gal	3 gal 2 qt	4 gal	4 gal 2 qt	5 gal
Nonfat Dry Milk	8 oz	1 lb	1 lb 8 oz	2 lb	2 lb 8 oz	3 lb	3 lb 8 oz	4 lb	4 lb 8 oz	5 lb
Chocolate Syrup	10 oz	1 pt 4 oz	1 qt	1 qt 8 oz	1 qt 16 oz	1 qt 24 oz	2 qt	2 qt 16 oz	2 qt 24 oz	3 qt

Nutrient Analysis per serving

Protein:	15 g
Carbohydrate:	26 g
Fat:	4 g
Sodium:	311 mg
Kilocalories:	256

Procedure

1. Combine all ingredients in mixing bowl. Mix until smooth.
2. Portion into 8 oz servings and serve immediately.

INGREDIENTS	10	20	30	40	50	60	70	80	90	100
Orange Juice Concentrate (from frozen)	1 qt 16 oz	3 qt	1 gal 16 oz	1 gal 2 qt	1 gal 3 qt	2 gal 1 qt	2 gal 2 qt	3 gal	3 gal 1 qt	3 gal 2 qt
Ice Cream	1 qt	2 qt	3 qt	1 gal	1 gal 1 qt	1 gal 2 qt	1 gal 3 qt	2 gal	2 gal 1 qt	2 gal 2 qt
Eggs	7	15	22	30	38	45	53	60	68	76

Nutrient Analysis per serving

Protein:	7 g
Carbohydrate:	26 g
Fat:	7 g
Sodium:	150 mg
Kilocalories:	202

Procedure

1. Combine all ingredients in mixing bowl. Mix until smooth.
2. Pour into 8 oz servings. Serve immediately.

PEANUT BUTTER MILKSHAKE

CATEGORY: *Supplement*   PORTION: *8 oz*

INGREDIENTS	10	20	30	40	50	60	70	80	90	100
Milk, whole	2 qt 12 oz	1 gal 24 oz	1 gal 3 qt	2 gal 2 qt	3 gal	3 gal 3 qt	4 gal 24 oz	4 gal 3 qt	5 gal 2 qt	6 gal
Peanut Butter	8 oz	1 lb	1 lb 8 oz	2 lb	2 lb 8 oz	3 lb	3 lb 8 oz	4 lb	4 lb 8 oz	5 lb
Bananas	10	20	30	40	50	60	70	80	90	100
Honey	¼ C	½ C	¾ C	1 C	1¼ C	1½ C	1¾ C	2 C	2¼ C	2½ C

Nutrient Analysis per serving

Protein:	13 g
Carbohydrate:	46 g
Fat:	18 g
Sodium:	201 mg
Kilocalories:	382

Procedure

1. Blend all ingredients and chill.

EGGNOG

INGREDIENTS	10	20	30	40	50	60	70	80	90	100
Nonfat Dry Milk	4 C	8 C	12 C	16 C	20 C	24 C	28 C	32 C	36 C	40 C
Water	2 qt 16 oz	5 qt	7 qt 16 oz	10 qt	12 qt 16 oz	4 gal	17 qt 16 oz	5 gal	22 qt 16 oz	25 qt
Eggs, fresh	10	20	30	40	50	60	70	80	90	100
Vanilla	½ C	1 C	1½ C	2 C	2½ C	3 C	3½ C	4 C	4½ C	5 C
Sugar, granulated	12 oz	1 lb	1 lb 8 oz	2 lb	2 lb 8 oz	3 lb	3 lb 8 oz	4 lb	4 lb 8 oz	5 lb

Nutrient Analysis per serving

Protein:	15 g
Carbohydrate:	51 g
Fat:	5 g
Sodium:	218 mg
Kilocalories:	340

Procedure

1. Combine nonfat dry milk and water. Place in large pan and scald to 145°F (use food thermometer).
2. Beat eggs, vanilla, and sugar together until smooth.
3. Add a little hot milk to this mixture, stirring constantly.
4. Add egg mixture to the milk and bring back to 145°F. Do not overheat or it will curdle.
5. Chill and serve.

BAKED POTATO TOPPER

INGREDIENTS	10	20	30	40	50	60	70	80	90	100
Sharp Cheese, shredded	8 oz	1 lb	1 lb 8 oz	2 lb	2 lb 8 oz	3 lb	3 lb 8 oz	4 lb	4 lb 8 oz	5 lb
Margarine, softened	½ C	1 C	1½ C	2 C	2½ C	3 C	3½ C	4 C	4½ C	5 C
Sour Cream	1 C	2 C	3 C	4 C	5 C	6 C	7 C	8 C	9 C	10 C
Green Onions or Chives	¼ C	½ C	¾ C	1 C	1¼ C	1½ C	1¾ C	2 C	2¼ C	2½ C
Bacon, cooked and crumbled	1 oz	2 oz	3 oz	4 oz	5 oz	6 oz	7 oz	8 oz	9 oz	10 oz

Nutrient Analysis per serving

Protein:	12 g
Carbohydrate:	1 g
Fat:	29 g
Sodium:	443 mg
Kilocalories:	322

Procedure

1. Whip together in mixer or food processor the cheese, soft margarine, sour cream, and green onions or chives.

Variation:

Mock Sour Cream: Cottage cheese and lemon juice may be substituted to make a lower cost, lower fat version of this topping.

CORNBREAD TOPPING FOR TURKEY PIE

CATEGORY: Topping   *PORTION: per serving*

INGREDIENTS	10	20	30	40	50	60	70	80	90	100
Cornmeal	4 oz	6 oz	8 oz	12 oz	14 oz	1 lb	1 lb 4 oz	1 lb 6 oz	1 lb 8 oz	1 lb 12 oz
Flour	4 oz	6 oz	8 oz	12 oz	14 oz	1 lb	1 lb 4 oz	1 lb 6 oz	1 lb 8 oz	1 lb 12 oz
Sugar	1 oz	2 oz	3 oz	4 oz	5 oz	6 oz	7 oz	8 oz	9 oz	10 oz
Baking Powder	1 oz	1 oz	2 oz	2 oz	3 oz	3 oz	4 oz	4 oz	5 oz	5 oz
Salt	¼ t	½ t	¾ t	1 t	1¼ t	1½ t	1¾ t	2 t	2¼ t	2½ t
Milk	6 oz	10 oz	1 pt	1 pt 4 oz	1 pt 8 oz	1 pt 12 oz	2 pt	2 pt 8 oz	2 pt 12 oz	3 pt
Eggs, beaten	1	2	3	4	5	6	7	8	9	10
Margarine, melted	1 T	2 T	3 T	4 T	5 T	6 T	7 T	8 T	9 T	10 T

Nutrient Analysis per serving

Protein:	2 g
Carbohydrate:	15 g
Fat:	2 g
Sodium:	227 mg
Kilocalories:	92

Procedure

1. Sift cornbread topping ingredients together. Add milk, beaten eggs, and melted margarine. Mix well.
2. Spoon topping over turkey pie. Bake at 400°F for about 30 minutes or until cornbread is done.

APPENDIX A   *Sample Cycle Menus*

MENU CYCLE I

WEEK I

	Monday	Tuesday	Wednesday	Thursday	Friday	Saturday	Sunday
Breakfast	Cranapple Juice Assorted Cereals Scrambled Eggs Bacon Toast, Margarine, Jelly Coffee, Tea, Milk	Orange Juice Assorted Cereals Country Sausage and Gravy Hot Biscuits, Butter, Jelly Coffee, Tea, Milk	Orange Juice Assorted Cereals Hotcakes with Syrup Crisp Bacon Coffee, Tea, Milk	Cranapple Juice Assorted Cereals Scrambled Eggs Bacon Sweet Roll or Danish Coffee, Tea, Milk	Orange Juice Assorted Cereals Fried Egg Sausage Links Toast, Margarine, Jelly Coffee, Tea, Milk	Orange-Pineapple Juice Assorted Cereals Hard-Boiled Eggs Bacon Doughnuts Coffee, Tea, Milk	Orange Juice Assorted Cereals Scrambled Eggs Bacon Toast, Margarine, Jelly Coffee, Tea, Milk
Lunch	Oven-Baked Pork Chop with Dressing (115)* Seasoned Green Peas and Cauliflower Apple Crumb Pie Garnish: Spiced Apple Ring	Taco Salad Southern Fruit Medley Chewy Bars (170)	Mushroom Steak (81) Oven Rice Pilaf (162) California Blend Vegetables Frozen Ice Cream Bar Garnish: Parsley	Tangy Baked Chicken (102) Seasoned Summer Squash (152) Skillet Green Beans (123) Roll and Butter Spiced Tomato Cake (183) Garnish: Tomato Wedge	Oven Broiled Fish Fillets (106) Spinach Soufflé (151) Baked Potato with Sour Cream Cherry Delight (169) Garnish: Lemon Wedge	Salmon Patties Macaroni and Cheese Seasoned Mixed Greens with Vinegar Apple Corn Muffin (35) Orange Sherbet Garnish: Tomato Wedge	Beef Pot Roast Au Jus Oven-Browned Potatoes (143) Baked Fresh Carrots (131) Angel Biscuit (34) Buttermilk Pie (168) Garnish: Parsley
Dinner	Homemade Vegetable Soup Peanut Butter and Jelly Sandwich Banana Old-Fashioned Oatmeal Cookie Garnish: Parsley HS: Cheese and Crackers and Fruit Juice**	Ham Loaf with Pineapple and Cherry (113) Au Gratin Potatoes Company Cabbage (129) Bread with Margarine Marshmallow Squares (177) HS: ½ banana and milk	Grilled Reuben Sandwich Potato Chips Sliced Tomatoes Rocky Road Pudding (181) Garnish: Pickle Spear HS: Sugar Cookies and Milk	Grilled Hot Dog and Bun Mustard and Relish Parmesan Pea Salad (61) Peaches Garnish: Parsley HS: Punch and Peanut Butter and Crackers	Cheeseburger Pie (73) Steamed Broccoli Spears Sliced Tomatoes Vinaigrette (65) Lime Jello with Pears Garnish: Pickle Spear HS: Hot Chocolate with Vanilla Wafers	Spaghetti Casserole (89) Seasoned Italian Vegetables Garden Salad with Oil and Vinegar Garlic Bread Fresh Fruit HS: Graham Crackers, Marsh- mallow Cream, Milk	Chicken Nuggets French Fries Frosted Lime Mold (57) Applesauce with Cinnamon HS: 6 oz Vanilla Milkshake

*Numbers in parentheses following recipe titles correspond to the pages on which the recipes appear.
**HS refers to a substantial bedtime snack.

WEEK II

	Monday	Tuesday	Wednesday	Thursday	Friday	Saturday	Sunday
Breakfast	Orange Juice Bacon Hot Cereal Hard-Boiled Eggs Toast, Butter, Jelly Milk	Orange Juice Scrambled Eggs Hot Cereal Hard-Boiled Eggs Toast, Butter, Jelly Milk	Orange-Pineapple Juice Dry Cereal Hot Cereal Fried Eggs Toast, Butter, Jelly Milk	Orange Juice Pancakes with Syrup Hot Cereal Hard-Boiled Eggs Toast, Butter, Jelly Milk	Cranapple Juice Scrambled Eggs Hot Cereal Hard-Boiled Eggs Toast, Butter, Jelly Milk	Orange Juice Doughnut Sausage Hot Cereal Hard-Boiled Eggs Toast, Butter, Jelly, Milk	Orange Juice Dry Cereal Hot Cereal Hard-Boiled Eggs Toast, Butter, Jelly Milk
Lunch	Mock Filet Mignon (80) Baked Potato with Sour Cream Peas and Mush- rooms (139) Southern Fruit Medley Milk Garnish: Parsley	Mustard Chicken (100) Lima Beans Beets with Pineap- ple (120) Mock English Triffle (178) Milk Garnish: Green Grapes	Oven-Broiled Fish Fillets (106) Au Gratin Spinach (149) Peppy Potatoes (144) Rosey Pears Milk Garnish: Lemon Slice on Fish	Veal Parmesan Spaghetti and Tomato Sauce Garlic Toast Fresh Fruit Milk Garnish: Parsley	Crusty Oven Baked Chicken (97) Cheese Grits (160) Buttered Whole Green Beans Biscuit with Butter Frozen Ambrosia (174) Milk Garnish: Tomato Wedge	Hero Sandwich Potato Chips Creamy Cucumber Salad (53) Peachy Cream Pudding (179) Milk Garnish: Pickle Spear	Crisp Baked Veal Squash Casserole #2 (154) Rosey Red Apples Roll and Butter Ice Cream with Caramel Sauce (189) Milk Garnish: Parsley
Dinner	Bacon-Wrapped Frank (108) Corn O'Brien (137) Sweet & Sour Green Beans (125) Milk Chocolate Ice Cream Garnish: Spiced Apple Rings HS: Crackers, Pea- nut Butter, Milk	Hamburger on Bun Frozen Mixed Vege- tables Potato Stixs Homemade Peanut Butter Cookie Milk Garnish: Lettuce and Tomato HS: 6 oz Milkshake	Pork Cutlet Supreme (117) Mashed Potatoes Succotash (124) Dream Salad (173) Bread and Butter Milk Garnish: Spiced Apple Rings HS: Fresh Fruit in Season and Milk	Beef Minute Steak Spanish Rice Buttered Brussel Sprouts Strawberry Hash (185) Bread and Butter Milk Garnish: Parsley HS: Cheese and Crackers and Juice	Baked Ham Slices (109) Broccoli Spears Mushroom Potatoes (142) Whole Wheat Muf- fin (41) Ice Cream Sand- wich Milk Garnish: Red Grapes HS: Doughnut and Milk	Cheese Casserole (104) Buttered Peas Fresh Fruit Cup (56) Milk Garnish: Parsley HS: Chocolate Chip Cookie and Milk	Freid Chicken Drumsticks Baked Beans Crunchy Garden Slaw on Leaf Lettuce (54) Fresh Fruit Angel Biscuit (34) Milk HS: Cheese and Crackers and Apple Juice

WEEK III

	Monday	Tuesday	Wednesday	Thursday	Friday	Saturday	Sunday
Breakfast	Cranapple Juice Sausage Links Hot Cereal with Bran Hard-Boiled Eggs Toast, Butter, Jelly Milk	Orange Juice Scrambled Eggs Hot Cereal with Bran Hard-Boiled Eggs Toast, Butter, Jelly Milk	Orange-Pineapple Juice Dry Cereal Hot Cereal with Bran Hard-Boiled Eggs Toast, Butter, Jelly Milk	Cranapple Juice Waffles and Syrup Hot Cereal Hard-Boiled Eggs Toast, Butter, Jelly Milk	Orange Juice Scrambed Eggs Hot Cereal Hard-Boiled Eggs Toast, Butter, Jelly, Milk	Orange-Pineapple Juice Doughnuts Bacon Hot Cereal with Bran Hard-Boiled Eggs Toast, Butter, Jelly Milk	Orange Juice Dry Cereal with Bran Hot Cereal Hard-Boiled Eggs Toast, Butter, Jelly Milk
Lunch	Chicken Tahitian (95) Rice Pilaf Baby Carrots Frozen Pudding Square (175) Garnish: Parsley	Roast Beef Twice-Baked Potatoes Peas with Pearl Onions Roll and Butter Buttermilk Pie (168) Garnish: Tomato Wedge	Stuffed Baked Potato with Ham and Cheese Broccoli Spears Whole Wheat Roll and Butter Bishop's Cake (167) Garnish: Spiced Apple Rings	Baked Fish Parisienne (105) Oven-Browned Potatoes (143) Baked Zucchini Banana Salad Dessert (166) Garnish: Lemon Wedge on leaf lettuce	Chicken Chop Suey Buttered Rice Marinated Carrots (59) Rainbow Sherbet Garnish: Parsley	Liver, Bacon, and Onions Whipped Potatoes Seasoned Green Beans Bread and Butter Chocolate Swirl Pudding Garnish: Tomato Wedge	Barbecued Short Ribs (68) Buttered New Potatoes Baked Broccoli (127) Brown and Serve Roll Plum Pudding Cake with Bran Garnish: Spiced Apple Rings
Dinner	Roast Pork Loin Yam Patties Broccoli-Corn Casserole Roll and Butter Honeybee Ambrosia (176) Garnish: Parsley HS: Vanilla Wafers and Milk	Turkey Salad Plate Potato Salad Spiced Beets and Onions Banana Bread with Bran Garnish: Parsley HS: Cheese and Crackers and Grape Juice	Chicken Breast Filet Calico Macaroni Salad (49) Cream Cheese Muffin (36) Sliced Tomatoes Chilled Peaches HS: ½ Banana, Milk	Sloppy Joes with Bun Criss-Cut Fries Tossed Salad with Italian Dressing Peanut Butter Bar with Bran Garnish: Pickle Spear HS: Peanut Butter and Crackers and Apple Juice	Country Sausage Burger with Biscuit (112) Home Fries Seasoned Spinach with Egg Slice Rosey Red Apples HS: Graham Crackers and Marshmallow Cream and Milk	Hot Ham & Cheese Sandwich (118) Baked Beans Hot Cabbage Slaw Molded Cherry Applesauce Gelatin Garnish: Parsley HS: Apple and Milk	Open-Faced Patty Melt (83) French Fries Mixed Fruit Salad Chocolate Oatmeal Cookies with Bran Garnish: French Fried Onion Ring HS: Hot Chocolate and Vanilla Wafers

MENU CYCLE II

WEEK I

	Monday	Tuesday	Wednesday	Thursday	Friday	Saturday	Sunday
Breakfast	Orange Juice Oatmeal with Raisins Scrambled Eggs Crisp Bacon Toast, Margarine, Jelly Coffee, Tea, Milk	Cranapple Juice Assorted Dry Cereals Diced Ham and Scrambled Eggs Toast, Margarine, Jelly Coffee, Tea, Milk	Apple Juice Cream of Wheat Hotcakes with Syrup Crisp Bacon Coffee, Tea, Milk	Orange Juice Assorted Dry Cereals Scrambled Egg Sausage Toast, Margarine, Jelly Coffee, Tea, Milk	Orange-Pineapple Juice Oatmeal with Cinnamon and Brown Sugar Boiled Egg Crisp Bacon Coffee, Tea, Milk	Orange Juice Assorted Dry Cereals Scrambled Egg Sausage Links Danish Coffee, Tea, Milk	Cranapple Juice Waffles with Syrup Crisp Bacon Assorted Dry Cereals Coffee, Tea, Milk
Lunch	Oven-Baked Pork Chops with Dressing (115) Herbed Green Beans Roll Cherry Cobbler Garnish: Tomato Slice on Leaf Lettuce	Old Fashioned Pot Roast (82) Oven-Browned Potatoes (143) Baked Fresh Carrots Honey Cornbread Oatmeal Pie Garnish: Parsley	Mustard Chicken (100) Cheese Potatoes (140) Peas and Mushrooms (139) Roll Strawberry Hash (185) Garnish: Tomato Wedge	Fried Fish with Tartar Sauce Duchess Potatoes (141) Broiled Tomatoes (157) Bread Mock English Trifle (178) Garnish: Lemon, Parsley	Fried Chicken Livers Mashed Potatoes with Cream Gravy Beets with Pineapple (120) Angel Biscuit (34) Bishop's Cake Garnish: Parsley	Pork Cutlet Supreme (117) Oven Rice Pilaf (162) Spinach Soufflé (151) Roll Buttermilk Pie (168) Garnish: Tomato Wedge	Crusty Oven-Baked Chicken (97) Succotash (124) French-Style Green Beans Tomatoes Vinaigrette on Leaf Lettuce (65) Biscuit Chocolate Mousse
Dinner	Old-Fashioned Chicken and Noodles (101) Country Spinach (150) Biscuit Fresh Fruit Cup (56) Garnish: Cranberry Relish HS: 4 oz Milk and Oatmeal Cookie	Homemade Vegetable Beef Soup Garden Cottage Cheese on Leaf Lettuce (58) Whole Wheat Muffin (41) Frozen Pudding Square (175) HS: 1 oz Cheese and 4 oz Fruit Juice	Bacon-Wrapped Franks (108) Corn Pudding (138) Crunchy Garden Slaw (54) Chewy Bars (170) Garnish: Parsley HS: 4 oz Milk and Vanilla Wafers	Ham Loaf with Glaze (113) Macaroni Salad Buttered Broccoli Spears Corn Muffin Cinnamon Applesauce HS: 2 T Peanut Butter and 2 Saltines and 4 oz milk	Pizzaburger (85) Tater Tots Emerald Isle Salad on Leaf Lettuce (55) Quick Cookies HS: 6 oz Strawberry Shake	Tomato-Celery Soup (47) Pimiento Cheese on Whole Wheat Spicy Fruit Compote (184) Brownie Garnish: Pickle Spear HS: Doughnut and Milk	Fish Square and Bun Tartar Sauce Pea and Cheese Salad (62) Harvard Beets Sherbet Garnish: Parsley HS: Graham Cracker and Milk

WEEK II

	Monday	Tuesday	Wednesday	Thursday	Friday	Saturday	Sunday
Breakfast	Orange Juice Grits Country Sausage and Gravy Biscuit, Margarine, Jelly Coffee, Tea, Milk	Apple Juice Oatmeal Scrambled Egg Crisp Bacon Toast, Margarine, Jelly Coffee, Tea, Milk	Cranapple Juice Assorted Dry Cereals Scrambled Egg Doughnut Coffee, Tea, Milk	Orange Juice Cream of Wheat Hard-Boiled Egg Sausage Toast, Margarine, Jelly	Orange-Pineapple Juice Assorted Dry Cereals Hotcakes with Syrup Crisp Bacon Coffee, Tea, Milk	Stewed Prunes Assorted Dry Cereals Scrambled Egg Sausage Links Coffee, Tea, Milk	Orange Juice Oatmeal Fried Egg on Biscuit Crisp Bacon Coffee, Tea, Milk
Lunch	Polish Sausage Sauerkraut Mashed Potatoes Cornbread and Butter Baked Apple Slices Garnish: Parsley	Roast Pork Sweet Potato Casserole (155) Seasoned Green Beans Roll and Butter Cheese Cake Garnish: Parsley	Gourmet Swiss Steak (77) Baked Potato Vegetable Medley Bran Muffin and Butter Fresh Fruit in Season Garnish: Parsley	Sautéed Beef Liver with Onions Potatoes O'Brien (146) Scalloped Cabbage (130) Bread and Butter Vanilla Ice Cream Garnish: Tomato Wedge	Baked Fish Parisienne (105) Parsley Potatoes Orange Beets Bread and Butter Strawberry Gelatin and Bananas	Barbecued Short Ribs (68) Hashbrown Potatoes Skillet Green Beans (123) Cornbread and Butter Lemon Meringue Pie Garnish: Parsley	Roast Turkey with Dressing Baked Broccoli Soufflé Roll and Butter Cranberry Delight Garnish: Spiced Apple Rings
Dinner	Mock Filet Mignon (80) Buttered New Potatoes in Jackets Mixed Vegetables Blueberry Muffin and Butter Assorted Gelatin Cubes Garnish: Onion Ring on Filet HS: 1 oz Cheese and Saltines and Juice	Creamed Mushroom Chicken with Biscuits (91) Buttered Peas Fruit and Melon Salad Sugar Cookies Garnish: Spiced Apple Rings HS: 6 oz Hot Chocolate	Cream of Vegetable Soup (44) Tuna Melt (107) Banana Salad on Leaf Lettuce (48) Vanilla Wafers HS: 2 T Peanut Butter and Saltines and 4 oz Juice	Oven-Fried Chicken Drumsticks Whole Kernel Corn Biscuit and Butter Peachy Cream Pudding (179) Garnish: Parsley HS: Sugar Cookie and 4 oz Milk	Cheeseburger Pie (73) Tossed Green Salad Toasted French Bread Rocky Road Pudding (181) Garnish: Parsley HS: 4 oz Milk and ½ Banana	Chicken Noodle Soup (42) Egg Salad on Whole Wheat with Leaf Lettuce Sliced Tomatoes Fruit Bars HS: 4 oz Milk and Muffin	Cheese Casserole (104) Broiled Tomatoes (157) Roll and Butter Frosted Lime Mold (57) Chocolate Chip Cookies Garnish: Parsley HS: 1 oz Cheese and Saltines and 4 oz Juice

WEEK III

	Monday	Tuesday	Wednesday	Thursday	Friday	Saturday	Sunday
Breakfast	Cranapple Juice Grits Scrambled Egg Canadian Bacon Toast, Margarine, Jelly Coffee, Tea, Milk	Orange Juice Assorted Dry Cereals French Toast with Syrup Sausage Coffee, Tea, Milk	Apple Juice Oatmeal with Brown Sugar Scrambled Egg Crisp Bacon Toast, Margarine, Jelly Coffee, Tea, Milk	Orange Juice Cream of Wheat Poached Egg Hot Biscuits, Honey Coffee, Tea, Milk	Grapefruit Juice Assorted Dry Cereals Scrambled Egg Crisp Bacon Toast, Margarine, Jelly Coffee, Tea, Milk	Orange Juice Oatmeal Scrambled Egg Sausage Toast, Margarine, Jelly Coffee, Tea, Milk	Orange-Pineapple Juice Assorted Dry Cereals Omelet Crisp Bacon Toasted English Muffin with Apple Butter Coffee, Tea, Milk
Lunch	Meatloaf (79) Cauliflower with Cheese Sauce Italian Zucchini Casserole (159) Roll and Butter Vanilla Pudding with Cherry Garnish: Parsley	Chicken Supreme (94) Yam Patties Buttered Broccoli Spears Cream Cheese Muf- fins and Butter (36) Lemon Sherbet Garnish: Parsley	Baked Ham Scalloped Potatoes (147) Buttered Turnip Greens Honey Cornbread and Butter Banana Pudding Garnish: Egg Slice on Greens	Crisp Baked Veal (74) Peppy Potatoes (144) Buttered Brussel Sprouts Roll and Butter Pineapple Upside- Down Cake Garnish: Radish Rose	Open-Faced Hot Roast Beef Sandwich Mashed Potatoes with Gravy Broiled Tomato Slice Chocolate Cream Pie	Oven Baked Fish Fillets Corn O'Brien (137) Buttered Peas Hush Puppies Angel Food Cake with Strawberries Garnish: Lemon Slice on Fish	Roast Corned Beef Buttered Potatoes Company Cabbage (129) Cornbread and Butter Gingerbread and Sauce Garnish: Apple Rings
Dinner	Hot Dog on Bun Baked Beans Potato Chips Fresh Fruit Cup (56) Garnish: Pickle Chips HS: 4 oz Milk and Vanilla Wafers	Baked Beef and Noodles Green Beans with Pimiento Angel Biscuit and Butter (34) Chocolate Cupcake with Frosting HS: 2 T Peanut Butter and Sal- tines and Juice	Salmon Croquettes Macaroni and Cheese Lima Beans Bread and Butter Honey Bee Ambro- sia (176) Garnish: Spiced Apple Rings HS: 4 oz Milk and Cookies	Curried Chicken with Broccoli (98) Wild Rice Whole Wheat Muf- fin and Butter (41) Chocolate Chip Cookies Garnish: Tomato Slice HS: 1 oz Cheese and Saltines and Juice	Cream of Potato Soup (43) Grilled Cheese Sandwich Carrifruit Salad (50) Marshmallow Squares Garnish: Parsley HS: Raisin Bread and 4 oz Milk	Pepper Steak (84) Holiday Broccoli Casserole (128) Summer Squash Bread and Butter Ice Cream Sundae Garnish: Tomato Wedge HS: 6 oz Hot Chocolate	Chicken Patty and Bun Steak Fries Seven-Layer Salad (64) Cherry Gelatin with Whipped Topping Garnish: Pickle Spear HS: 4 oz Milk and Graham Cracker

APPENDIX B   *Dietary Exchanges*

Cooking with Dried Eggs

Dried eggs are whole shell eggs that have been processed to remove the water and leave the solid particles in powder form. This powdered form of eggs can be easily restored for use in cooking by adding water in the following proportions:

Dried whole egg	+ Water	= Whole shell egg
¼ C egg mix	¼ C water	1 whole egg
½ C egg mix	½ C water	2 whole eggs
¾ C egg mix	¾ C water	3 whole eggs
1½ C egg mix ·	1½ C water	6 whole eggs

To measure dried eggs accurately, sift powdered eggs once, then measure, leveling the surface.

After the cans of dried eggs are opened, they should be used immediately. If not used immediately, they should be emptied into a glass jar and covered tightly. Store in a cool place, preferably the refrigerator.

Dried eggs must be mixed with water when used in cooking. They are usually mixed with water before mixing with other ingredients. When recipes call for sifting or mixing the dry ingredients, the dried eggs can be mixed with these and water added with the liquid.

Follow these directions for mixing powder eggs with water:

1. Sift egg powder once, before measuring.

2. Use cool or barely lukewarm water.

3. Pour the water in a deep bowl. Never use a straight-sided pan.

4. Sprinkle measured powder over water all at one time.

Remember that dried eggs should be cooked thoroughly before eating.

Information courtesy of USDA.

Dehydrated, Instant Mashed Potatoes

The Dehydrated, Instant Mashed Potatoes now being offered by the Department of Agriculture are in two forms: flakes and granules. The potatoes have been cooked, mashed, and dehydrated, resulting in a product not to exceed 8 percent moisture.

The potato flakes and granules are packed in cartons, bags, pouches, or No. 10 cans.

Flakes are packed in 5 lb. (80 oz.) (2.26 kg) containers with 6 containers (30 lb.) (13.6 kg) per case.

Granules are packed in 5 lb. (80 oz.) (2.26 kg) containers with 6 containers (30 lb.) (13.6 kg) per case, or in 6 lb. (96 oz.) (2.72 kg) No. 10 cans with 6 containers (36 lb.) (16.3 kg) per case.

STORAGE

Store both forms of instant potatoes in cool, dry place at 32°F to 70°F. Store opened potatoes in a refrigerator in air-tight containers.

NUTRITIVE VALUE

Dehydrated potatoes have been fortified with both vitamins A and C. One ounce of potato granules or flakes contains at least 1,000 International Units of vitamin A and at least 36 mg of vitamin C. Nutrition information (courtesy of USDA) per ⅔ oz dry (makes ½ cooked):

calories	80	carbohydrate	17 grams
protein	2 grams	fat	0 grams

Percent of U.S. Recommended Allowances (USRDA):

protein	2	riboflavin	0
vitamin A	15	niacin	4
vitamin C	40	calcium	0
thiamine	0	iron	0

TABLE B-1   Yield Information on Dehydrated Potatoes (Flakes and Granules) as Described in the Previous Section

Food as Purchases (1)	Purchases (2)	Unit Servings Per (3)	Serving Size/Portion (4)	Purchase Units For (5)	Additional Yield Information (6)
POTATOES, WHITE *Dehydrated Low Moisture*					
Flakes	No. 10 cans (40 oz)	60.70 121.40	½ C reconstituted ¼ C reconstituted	1.65 .82	
	5 lb pkg.	121.40 242.80	½ C reconstituted ¼ C reconstituted	.82 .41	
	Pound*	24.30 48.60	½ C reconstituted ¼ C reconstituted	4.15 2.10	
Granules	No. 10 cans (96 oz)	145.00 290.00	½ C reconstituted ¼ C reconstituted	.69 .35	
	5 lb pkg.	121.40 242.80	½ C reconstituted ¼ C reconstituted	.82 .41	
	Pound	24.80 48.60	½ C reconstituted ¼ C reconstituted	4.15 2.10	1 lb dry = about 2¼ C

*One pound of dry flakes yields a considerably greater volume than one pound of dry granules.

Preparing Instant
Mashed Potatoes (flakes)

For best results, prepare in small batches as needed. Mix in the serving
container or counter pans (12" × 20" × 6" approximate). *For best results,
use of a mixer is discouraged. Overmixing should be avoided.*

TABLE B-2

INGREDIENTS	100 Servings		120 Servings	
	Weights	*Measures*	*Weights*	*Measures*
Boiling Water		2 gal 1 qt*		2 gal 2½ qt*
Warm Milk		3 qt		1 gal
Butter or margarine	11 oz	1⅓ C	14 oz	1¾ C
Salt	1¾ oz	2 T	2 oz	3 T
Potato Flakes	4 lb 2 oz		5 lb	

*Since the starch content of potatoes can differ, adjustment of the liquid may be necessary. Increase or decrease the quantity of liquid as needed for a fluffy product.

Directions

1. Combine water, milk, butter or margarine, and salt. Stir to melt margarine.
2. Divide these; combine ingredients into two batches (preferably 2 serving counter pans).
3. Pour ½ of potato flakes into each container of liquid mixture.
4. Stir ½ to 1 minute to moisten. Stir an additional ½ to 1 minute until fluffy.
5. Serve with #8 scoop (½ C).

TIP FOR KEEPING WARM: Warm in compartment steamer for a nice, moist, fluffy product. For best results mix in batches and avoid holding product more than ½ hour.

SERVINGS: ½ C provides ½ C vegetable.

Nonfat Dry Milk Fortified with Vitamins A and D

INGREDIENTS

PACK SIZE: 50 lb bags

Dried Pasteurized skim milk enriched with Vitamins A and D. May have anti-oxidant added.

YIELD

One pound of nonfat dry milk will yield 18.2 C of fluid milk when reconstituted. One pound is equivalent to 3.78 C powder.

USES

Nonfat dry milk may be reconstituted with water and made into a liquid for use in dishes such as soups, gravies, sauces, and custards. It may be used in place of fresh milk in recipes requesting milk.

STORAGE

Nonfat dry milk stores best when tightly covered, kept cool and dry, and off the floor. When exposed to the air, it becomes lumpy and the flavor changes. The chart shows maximum storage periods (in months) at different temperatures and amounts of humidity.

	100°F	70°F	40°F	0°F
60 percent humidity	2	5	10	20
40 percent humidity	5	9	15	30

NUTRITIONAL VALUE

1 cup of nonfat dry milk provides 436 calories:

protein	43.1 g	riboflavin	2.16 mg
carbohydrate	62.8 g	niacin	1.1 mg
fat	1.0 g	sodium	638 mg
iron	0.7 mg	potassium	2,094 mg
Vitamin A	2,650 IU	calcium	1,570 mg
ascorbic acid	9 mg	phosphorus	1,219 mg
thiamin	0.42 mg		

(Agriculture Handbook #456)

Information courtesy of USDA.

PREPARATION

When recipes requesting milk contain a large portion of dry ingredients, as for bread, biscuits, muffins, and cakes, nonfat dry milk may be mixed with the other dry ingredients. For uniform results with recipes, weigh rather than measure nonfat dry milk. Use as directed in recipes requiring dry milk or as a substitute when fresh milk is requested.

Reconstituting Nonfat Dry Milk

Check the package to determine whether it is instant or noninstant.

Makes 1 cup of milk

NFDM, Instant   ⅓ C
Water, Cold   1 C

1. Add NFDM to water.
2. Stir to mix.

NFDM, Non-instant   ⅓ C
Water, Warm   1 C

1. Make a paste with NFDM and small amount of water.
2. Gradually add remaining water.

OR

1. Add NFDM to water, whip, beat, or shake vigorously.

Makes 1 gal of milk

NFDM, Instant   5⅓ C
Water, Cold   1 gal

1. Add NFDM to water.
2. Stir to mix.

NFDM, Non-instant   3¼ C
Water, Warm   1 gal

1. Make a paste with NFDM and small amount of water.
2. Gradually add remaining water.

OR

1. Add NFDM to water, whip, beat, or shake vigorously.

Conversion of Recipes to Diabetic Exchanges

Recipes not listed are considered unsuitable for diabetic diets.

RECIPE	EXCHANGES
Cornbread Topping for Turkey Pie	1 bread
Beef Pot Pie	2 medium fat meat, ½ bread, 1 fat
Parmesan Pea Salad	½ medium fat meat, 1 bread, 2 fat
Italian Tomato Soup	1 bread, ½ fat
Spinach Soufflé	2 bread
Banana Salad Dessert	2 bread, 2 fat
Turkey Pie	3 medium fat meat, 2 bread
Beefy Macaroni Casserole	3 medium fat meat, 1 bread
Curried Chicken with Broccoli	4 medium fat meat, 1 fat, 1 vegetable
Green Bean Casserole	1 vegetable
Prune Coffee Cake	1 bread, ½ fat
Boiled Dinner	2 medium fat meat, 1 bread
Marinated Carrots	1 bread, 1 vegetable, 1 fat
Spicy Fruit Compote	1 fruit
Creamed Mushroom Chicken with Biscuits (without biscuits)	2 medium fat meat, ½ bread, 1 fat
Tangy Baked Chicken	4 lean meat, 1 bread
Crusty Oven-Baked Chicken	3 lean meat, 1 fat
Chicken Tahitian	4 medium fat meat
Chicken Supreme	3 medium fat meat, 1 bread, 2 fat
Tuna Melt	2 high fat meat, 1 fat, 1 bread
Open-Faced Patty Melt	2 high fat meat, 1 bread, 1 fat
Oven Rice Pilaf	1 bread, 1 fat
Chicken Pot Pie with Batter Crust	2 high fat meat, 1½ bread, 1 fat
Baked Fish Parisienne	2½ medium fat, 1 bread, 2 fat

RECIPE	EXCHANGES
Chicken Noodle Soup	2 lean meat, ½ bread, 1 vegetable, 2 fat
One-Cup Salad	1 fruit, 1 fat
Fresh Fruit Cup	1 fruit
Spanish Baked Steak	3 lean meat, 1 vegetable, 1 fat
Crisp Baked Veal	3 medium fat, 2 fat
Oven-Baked Pork Chop with Dressing	3 high fat meat, 1 bread, 1 fat
Chicken and Rice	4 lean meat, 1 bread
Pepper Steak	2 medium fat meat, 2 vegetables
Squash Casserole #2	1 bread, 2 fat
Italian Zucchini Casserole	1 vegetable, 1½ fat
Creamy Cucumber Salad	1 vegetable, 2 fat
Scalloped Tomatoes	1 bread, 1 fat
Pizzaburgers	2 high fat meat, 2 bread
Creamed Mushroom Chicken with Biscuits	3 lean meat, ½ bread, 1 fat
Cube Steak Italiano	3 high fat meat, ½ bread, 1 fat
Pumpkin Nut Bread	2 bread, 1 fat
Tomato-Celery Soup	2 vegetables
Frozen Ambrosia	1 bread, 2 fat
Green Beans Au Gratin	1 vegetable
Peppy Potatoes	2 bread, 1 fat
Baked Broccoli	1 vegetable, 1 medium fat meat
Spicy Fruit Compote	1 fruit
Hungarian-Style Pork Cutlet	3 high fat meat, ½ bread, 1 fat
Cheese Potatoes	2 bread, 1 medium fat meat
Mustard Chicken	5 lean meat, 1 fat
Three-Bean Medley	2 vegetables
Corn O'Brien	1½ bread, 1 fat
Green Bean Casserole	1 vegetable
Duchess Potatoes	1½ bread, 2 fat
Potatoes O'Brien	1 bread, 3 fat
Cheeseburger Pie	3 high fat meat, ½ bread

RECIPE	EXCHANGES
Calico Macaroni Salad	1 bread, 1 high fat meat, 2 fats
Meatloaf	3 medium fat meat, ½ bread, 1 fat
Ham Loaf (no glaze)	2 high fat meat, 1 bread
Beef Steak Patties	5 medium fat meat
Squash Casserole #1	1 vegetable, 1½ high fat meat, 1 fat
Peas and Mushrooms	1 vegetable
Apple Corn Muffins	1 bread, 1 fat
Pumpkin Muffins	1½ bread, 1 fat
Scalloped Cabbage	1 high fat meat, ½ bread
Skillet Green Beans	1 vegetable, 1 fat
Country Sausage Burger	2 high fat meat, 2 bread, 1 fat
Salisbury Steak Italiano	3 medium fat meat, 1 bread
Deviled Beef Patties	3 medium fat meat, 1 fat
Pork Cutlets Supreme	3 high fat meat, 1 bread
Mock Filet Mignon	3 medium fat meat, ½ bread, 1 fat
Tomatoes Vinaigrette	1 vegetable, 2 fat
Corn Pudding	1 lean meat, 2 bread
Navy Bean Soup (1 C)	1 lean meat, 1 bread, 1 fat
Carrifruit Salad (½ C)	2 fruit
Cream of Potato Soup	2 bread, 1½ fat
Chicken Noodle Soup (1 C)	4 medium fat meat, 1 bread
Lyonnaise Carrots	1 vegetable, 1 fat
Honey Cornbread	3 bread, 1 fat
Oven-Fried Pork Chop	3 medium fat meat
Frozen Pudding Square (low calorie pudding)	1 milk, 1 fruit
Cream Cheese Muffins	2 fat, 2 bread
Curried Chicken with Broccoli	4 lean meat, 1 vegetable, 3 fat
Seasoned Summer Squash	1 vegetable
Honey Bee Ambrosia	1 fruit (if replace honey with artificial sweetener)
Angel Biscuit	1 bread, 2 fat

RECIPE	EXCHANGES
Whole Wheat Muffin	2 bread, 1 fat
Pea and Cheese Salad	1 high fat meat, ½ bread, 1½ fat
Garden Cottage Cheese	1 lean meat, 1 fat (if use low fat cottage cheese)
Oven-Browned Potatoes	1 bread, 2 fat
Holiday Broccoli Casserole	1 vegetable, 1 fat, ½ bread
Mushroom Steak	2¼ high fat meat
Cheese Casserole	2 high fat meat, 1 bread, 1 fat
Succotash	2 bread
Country Spinach	1 vegetable, 1 bread, 1 fat
Cream of Vegetable Soup	1 bread, 1 fat
Potato Cheese Puff	1 bread, 1 fat
Baked Ham Slice	2 lean meat
Old-Fashioned Chicken and Noodles	3 lean meat, ½ bread
Oven-Broiled Fish Fillets	2 lean meat
Seven-Layer Salad	1 vegetable, 2 fat
Crunchy Garden Slaw	2 vegetable, 1 fat (if use low calorie salad dressing)
Corn Fritters	2 bread, 1 medium fat meat
Glazed Carrots	1 vegetable (if made with artificial sweetener)
Mushroom Potatoes	1 bread, 1 fat
Company Cabbage	1 vegetable
Beets with Pineapple	1½ bread (if use artificial sweetener)
Broiled Tomatoes	1 vegetable, 1 fat (if made with diet mayonnaise)
Gourmet Swiss Steak	3 lean meat, 1 vegetable, 1 fat
Irish Stew	2 bread, 2 vegetable, 3 lean meat
Marinated Carrots	1 bread, 1 vegetable, 1 fat
Crispy Baked Chicken	4 lean meat, 1½ bread, 3 fat
Scalloped Potatoes	1 medium fat meat, 1½ bread
Au Gratin Spinach	1 high fat meat, 1 bread
Old-Fashioned Pot Roast	3 medium fat meat, 2 bread, 1 fat
Three-Bean Medley	1 bread

RECIPE	EXCHANGES
Spiced Tomato Cake	1½ bread, 1 fat
Savory Steak	3 medium fat meat, 1 bread, 3½ fat
Corn Pudding	2 high fat meat, 1 bread, 1 fat
Mustard Chicken	4 lean meat, 3 fat
Texas Rice	1 bread, 1 fat
Salisbury Steak	3 medium fat meat, ½ bread, 1 fat
Cauliflower au Gratin	1 medium fat meat, ½ bread, 1 fat
Hot Ham and Cheese Sandwich	2 medium fat meat, 1½ bread, 2 fat
Scalloped Potatoes with Cheese	1 high fat meat, 1 bread
Spaghetti Casserole	2 medium fat meat, 1 bread, ½ fat
Pineapple Cottage Cheese	½ medium fat meat, 1 bread, 3 fat
Oven Rice Pilaf	1 bread, 1 fat

INDEX